How to Be Really F*cking Good at Manifesting Abundance

A simple, no-BS approach to reaching your greatest potential, manifesting success, wealth, and love, and discovering your true inner happiness

Aimee Alexandra Marshall

© **Copyright 2021 - All rights reserved.**

The content contained within this book may not be reproduced, duplicated or transmitted without direct written permission from the author or the publisher.

Under no circumstances will any blame or legal responsibility be held against the publisher, or author, for any damages, reparation, or monetary loss due to the information contained within this book, either directly or indirectly.

Legal Notice:

This book is copyright protected. It is only for personal use. You cannot amend, distribute, sell, use, quote or paraphrase any part, or the content within this book, without the consent of the author or publisher.

Disclaimer Notice:

Please note the information contained within this document is for educational and entertainment purposes only. All effort has been executed to present accurate, up to date, reliable, complete information. No warranties of any kind are declared or implied. Readers acknowledge that the author is not engaged in the rendering of legal, financial, medical or professional advice. The content within this book has been derived from various sources. Please consult a licensed professional before attempting any techniques outlined in this book.

By reading this document, the reader agrees that under no circumstances is the author responsible for any losses, direct or indirect, that are incurred as a result of the use of the information contained within this document, including, but not limited to, errors, omissions, or inaccuracies.

Table of Contents

INTRODUCTION 1

CHAPTER 1: DEFINE SUCCESS 7
    YOU ARE UNIQUE 9
    LEARNING THROUGH FAILURE 10
    BELIEVE IN YOURSELF 11
    IS THE TIMING RIGHT? 14
    STOP COMPARING 15
    THE VISUALIZATION PROCESS 16

CHAPTER 2: HOW THE HELL DID I GET HERE? 19
    REGAINING YOUR IDENTITY 20
    WHERE DO LIMITING BELIEFS COME FROM 22
    TAKING THE ROAD LESS TRAVELLED 23
    WHAT'S HOLDING YOU BACK? 25
    STICK WITH IT! 28

CHAPTER 3: BELIEVING THE LIES 29
    THE TOXIC LIES WE TELL OURSELVES 30
        My Age is Against Me 30
        The Timing Just Isn't Right 31
        Believing You Don't Deserve to Achieve Your Goals 32
        Success Is Meant for Others 33
        Success Isn't Possible 34
        I'm Going to Fail 35
        Nobody Cares if I Succeed or Fail 35
    SET YOUR STANDARD AND RAISE THE BAR 36

CHAPTER 4: DEALING WITH THE BS 41
    BECOME ACCOUNTABLE FOR THE BS 41
    SEE THROUGH THE BS 43
    ACCEPT THAT LIFE IS MESSY 45

GET OVER THE DRAMA OF TOXIC PEOPLE 47
TAKING THE NEXT STEPS 48

CHAPTER 5: TAKING NAMES AND KICKING ASS 51

HOW OUR PAST BELIEFS AFFECT US NOW 52
THE POWER OF NEGATIVITY..53
OVERCOME NEGATIVE THINKING 55
THE POSITIVE PEOPLE IN YOUR LIFE..57
RECLAIM YOUR POWER..58

CHAPTER 6: FACING FEAR 61

FACE UP TO YOUR FEARS..63
MAKING A CHANGE...64
TAKE ACTION 66
CREATE A ROUTINE AROUND REACHING YOUR GOALS 69

.CHAPTER 7: LIVING THE LAW 71

WHAT IS THE LAW OF ATTRACTION 73
WHERE DOES THE LAW OF ATTRACTION COME FROM? 75
VIBRATIONAL ENERGY AND FREQUENCIES..76
VISUALIZE AND STATE YOUR INTENTIONS..79

CHAPTER 8: LOVING YOURSELF 83

STOP COMPARING YOURSELF 84
LET GO OF FEAR 85
BE KIND TO YOURSELF...87
TAKE CHARGE 89
LIFE YOURSELF UP 91
PUT YOURSELF FIRST...93

CHAPTER 9: HEALTHY HABITS 97

HOW HABITS ARE DEVELOPED OVER TIME...97
CHANGING YOUR HABITS TO BUILD A HEALTHY LIFESTYLE......................99
CHANGE WON'T COME EASY 101
KEEP YOUR MOOD AND HEALTH IN CHECK 104
TRY NEW THINGS 106
BE MINDFUL OF YOUR THOUGHTS 109

CHAPTER 10: MANIFESTING ABUNDANCE 111

LIVING A LIFE OF ABUNDANCE 112
THERE'S POWER IN THINKING POSITIVELY...113

VISUALIZE YOUR GOALS AND MANIFEST THEM 116
BELIEVE THAT YOU ARE WORTHY OF ABUNDANCE 118

CONCLUSION 121

REFERENCES 125

"Whatever we are waiting for—peace of mind, contentment, grace, the inner awareness of simple abundance—it will surely come to us, but only when we are ready to receive it with an open and grateful heart."
-Sarah Ban Breathnach

Introduction

Have you ever sat back, looked at your life, and asked what the hell am I doing here? How come there are so many other people that seem to have everything? It's not fair, right? Deep down, you know that life's never been fair from the get-go. It just so happens that you're feeling it now more than ever.

Maybe someone in your office has just been promoted ahead of you when you deserved the promotion instead? You might still associate with friends from school, and they all look super successful. They seem to have the ideal spouse who's super supportive, the perfect house, the perfect children, complete with the ideal, well-behaved, and fully house-trained pets.

This constant comparison can be physically draining and emotionally exhausting. You keep on going through your head. What could you have done differently? Where the hell did things start going so completely pear-shaped that it all went to hell in a handbasket?

You may have already bought and read a stack of books on manifesting abundance before. There they are, all gathering dust because you read through the first couple of pages, and then it happened—the book became too scientific or technical for you to understand. You found yourself having to wade through the same old bullshit that's spewed out of the mouths of all of these seemingly innocent authors.

Now, don't get me wrong, there are some excellent books out there that have merit and could offer you some of the tools that we're going to work through as part of this book. The main difference is that you're not going to have to sift through all the BS to get there. Whatever has attracted you to this particular book at this stage in your life is just the way it should be. Something is resonating deep within your soul right now.

Each section of this book is divided so that it's easy to relate to, and the solutions are simple enough to start applying to your life. Instead of looking only at the "here and now," you're actually considering your future. There are so many approaches that you can implement into your life immediately.

My main aim with this book is to help you find the best and shortest possible route to achieving your full potential. It's showing you how to do it without having to make too many sacrifices to your current life and lifestyle. My goal is to help you implement each of these changes that will lead you to true and lasting happiness. Not just surface happiness that doesn't last because it's as plastic as that AMEX card you carry in your wallet. Some of the things we are going to discuss as we look at some creative ways to attract abundance, wealth, success, and happiness include the following:

- Manifesting abundance

- Reaching your greatest potential

- Manifesting success

- Attracting success, wealth, and love into your life

- Finding inner peace and happiness

The key takeaway is learning to use some simple, practical tools that you can apply to your day-to-day life immediately to help you achieve what you want out of life.

Hopefully, the examples I'm going to use are simple enough that you can see exactly how they can add value to your life. After all, that's what you're looking for, aren't you? You want to make changes to your life that are lasting. You want to regain control of yourself and your life after something negative has turned your world upside down.

No matter where you've been in the past or how many times you've failed, there's always time to try again. If you happen to be holding this book in your hands or listening to it, then you are already halfway there. You can start by ignoring those nagging voices in your head. Get stuck into HOW TO BE REALLY F*CKING GOOD AT MANIFESTING ABUNDANCE: A SIMPLE, NO-BS APPROACH TO REACHING YOUR GREATEST POTENTIAL, MANIFESTING SUCCESS, WEALTH, AND LOVE, AND DISCOVERING YOUR TRUE INNER HAPPINESS. I guarantee this is going to be one hell of a ride. If you are unsure whether this book is for you, I dare you to keep on reading or listening.

Do not get stuck in the quagmire of mediocrity. There are enough mediocre people out there who spend their lives wandering aimlessly. They have no clue where they are going or what they want to get out of life. That is not you, though! You have almost made your decision. So, what is it going to take for you to turn the page? The reality is that without turning the page, you'll never really know if this is the right book for you. It may be what you've been looking for.

My main aim is to offer you tools that you can apply to your life immediately, without having to get a master's degree in manifesting abundance. You can make these changes that offer you real results and quickly. It is also to keep you motivated throughout this process so that you aren't tempted to put it down like others that you may have already tried.

Let's face it, who doesn't want a life that's way better than what they have at the moment. I don't think that any of us can ever say that we're 100% happy with what we have; this doesn't always have to be materialistic things, either. I'm talking about things like happiness, love, and a life that makes you feel fulfilled. What could be more important than that?

Without leaving anything more to chance, it's time to take your life back and get manifesting abundance! You can do it. It all starts with you, and it all starts now.

"Success is not measured by what you accomplish, but by the opposition you have encountered, and the courage with which you have maintained the struggle against overwhelming odds."
-Orison Swett Marden

Chapter 1:

Define SUCCESS

Defining success is one of the most challenging things to do because it means something entirely different for each individual. What success means to you and what it means to me are possibly complete opposites. I may be chasing fame and fortune, whereas these two things may be at the bottom of your bucket list. Instead, you may want a loving and lasting relationship with someone who's genuine and loves you just the way you are. Maybe you want to be excellent at your job so that you get promoted to the corner office with the fancy title on the door and magnificent view of the city.

Whatever success means to me and what it means to the person next door is completely irrelevant. The world portrays success as flawless beauty, the perfect figure, the perfect spouse, and home, complete with perfect children. It's living in an upscale neighborhood where status and luxury are key to fitting in with the popular kids, and adults for that matter. Are you having some flashbacks to when you were in high school or maybe even college?

It's just one of those things that there will always be the haves and the have nots. You simply need to make a conscious decision as to whether you're still going to let childish popularity contests rule your life at this moment.

If this is where you happen to find yourself, then the only person who can decide to change is you. Have you ever taken some time out to sit and think about what you want out of life? What do you want your future to look like? I've already mentioned that what motivates one individual is not always the same for someone else.

Set aside enough time where you aren't going to be interrupted for a couple of hours. Take a pen and paper and let your mind freely wander as you fill pages with everything you've ever dreamed about having, becoming, owning, or doing with your life. As mentioned before, it doesn't matter if what you want happens to be fame, fortune, and materialistic things as long as you're realistic about it.

Unrealistic thoughts are part of the problem and why people often fail to manifest things for their lives. Firstly, their goals and dreams are entirely unrealistic, making it impossible to achieve what they want out of life. Next, they don't believe that they deserve to have any of the things they've written down. Deep down, you know that this is not true; however, as long as you don't believe you're worthy of your goals, you're setting yourself up for failure, time, and time, again.

You don't need to have the same goals as the jock or cheerleader you grew up with. The world would be a boring place if we were each working toward the same thing. The things you want should make you feel comfortable in your own skin. If your goals don't align with others, even those closest to you, that's quite okay. Don't be put off by this. Remember that it's your life, after all, and each of the things you aspire to should hold special meaning to you. You're looking for those things that will propel you closer toward the ultimate dream you have for your life. You are the only one who knows what this success looks like. Sure, those around you may even try to influence you or prompt you to change who you are and even alter the direction your life is moving in. Despite them being influential, motivational, or even successful themselves doesn't mean you need to adopt any of their goals as your own.

You Are Unique

Remember, you are unique, special, and completely your own person. Sure, you belong to the human race. You are part of the nationality of a country and even a family. This doesn't mean anything when it comes to who you are or who you want to be as an individual. To be truly authentic to who you are, you need to be living your own life rather than the life of someone else. Those who aren't authentic to themselves are usually desperately unhappy.

As an individual, you should be able to define your own success without being forced into someone else's idea of what you should be doing; this sometimes happens when we are children. Parents, grandparents, and other family members may have all chosen a specific path. Your family's decisions may have worked extremely well for them, but it doesn't mean it's ideal for you. An example of this would be coming from a family of doctors. You may have an aversion to blood. Instead of choosing this route, you may be drawn to electronics or want to make a career out of doing something creative instead. Achieving success isn't chasing someone else's dream—you have to have your own dreams.

Imagine success as finally reaching the pinnacle of your personal mountain that you need to climb. The problem is that unless you know which mountain yours is, you may be climbing forever. It's challenging to reach the precipice if you aren't convinced you're on the right path. You should be the one in control of your destiny. Figure out exactly where that is. Following the roadmap provided by someone else will not get you to where you need to be.

It's perfectly fine if your goals and dreams aren't status orientated or focused on money. What's important is that you discover what excites you and what you're passionate about. Finding your passion will help you inch that much closer to exactly where you want to be. You'll never truly appreciate anything that you've worked toward unless you're passionate about it. Without this crucial ingredient, your success will feel empty, it may feel forced, and you may not even feel as though you've achieved anything worthwhile.

Learning Through Failure

Part of being successful is learning that failure is part of the process. If we never fail, we can never experience true success. Failure means learning and growing. We'll never be excellent at something without trial and error. There will always be a starting point before you can truly become a master at something. Failing brings the opportunity to learn new things, especially what to avoid doing in the future.

Take, for example, a baby learning to walk for the first time. There's a lot of work going into being able to find the right balance. The right balance usually comes with learning how to pull themselves up against something first. It means needing a crutch of some description. Does this mean that the baby is weak? Not at all. It just means that learning is part of the process.

Similarly, we may need to lean on others for us to grow and develop. In many instances, these could be those in the same field who have already made it. We can use them to teach, coach, and mentor us. We are learning from them as to what path to follow and what pitfalls to avoid. It doesn't help us grow and develop when we are petrified of making a mistake. These mistakes will prove to be priceless in learning how to move forward successfully.

Sometimes we see failure as weakness, but it's how we learn. High expectations are great, but they need to be realistic. You'd never attempt a triathlon or ultra-marathon without investing the right amount of time in training, changing your diet, and completing several other events successfully. It takes time, effort, and energy. Becoming successful at anything in life requires each of these key elements.

How will you know what you're passionate about if you're not even sure of who you are? The secret to discovering your passion is attempting new things often. How will you know whether you're creative or excellent with numbers unless you try? Maybe you'll win, and maybe you'll lose, but that's all part of figuring out what you want out of life. Once you can identify what that is, it becomes easier for you to achieve the success you deserve.

Believe in Yourself

Often, our journey toward success is hampered with self-doubt and anticipating failure at every turn, rather than visualizing success. Let's face it, a lot of what we tell ourselves determines whether we fail or succeed. There's a lot to be said about how we perceive success in our lives. Are we setting ourselves up to win because we believe we deserve only the best, or are we already anticipating failure?

John Herbert Phillips, a high school superintendent, made the following statement during several addresses to high school students in 1905.

> *"Have faith in yourself; develop confidence in your own power, reliance on your own resources. If you believe you can, you will; if you think you can't, you will fail. There is much truth in the old Latin motto: "Possunt quia posse videntur." They can, because they think they can"* (Phillips, 1905).

Believing in yourself and your potential is another vital ingredient that can lead to success. You will never experience any degree of success when you're filled with self-doubt. In fact, self-doubt is the antithesis of being successful. Believing in your skills, abilities, and talents will allow you to experience these results for yourself. By giving it your all consistently, it's safe to say that the success you're looking for will manifest in your life.

The main focus of this book is to manifest abundance. One of the ways to do this is by recognizing that it is all around you. There's no difference when it comes to success. When you can acknowledge that there are endless opportunities around you and different things you can try, it becomes easier to adopt the right mindset. This mindset or belief system is one of success rather than failure.

It helps you see an abundance rather than a lack thereof. It's human nature to automatically default to a shortage mentality rather than one of abundance. The truth is that as we recognize the endless abundance and opportunities around us, it becomes so much easier for us to identify and set worthwhile goals to work toward. We have to be able to set each of these goals for ourselves and then break them down into smaller steps to achieve the ultimate reward. Breaking these down is like climbing that mountain. You have to do it one step at a time by placing one foot in front of the other.

Some of the things we may be pursuing could be status symbols; maybe you want to have enough money to live the life of your dreams. Perhaps it's not even directed at yourself. You may be driven to being able to make a difference in the lives of others. I know of some individuals who spend most of their time helping those in need worldwide. Some may feel that this is a bit extreme and prefer to focus their attention closer to home and provide their children with all the opportunities they never had growing up.

Whatever your yardstick for measuring success, it's only you that can decide what success looks like to you. You have to determine what will motivate you and keep you motivated to keep doing what you're doing. Your motivation can often be clouded by snags, obstacles, and even significant failures. Don't let this distract you from continuing toward the dreams you have for yourself. No amount of failure should get you to throw in the towel, especially not when you're pursuing something that gets you excited about getting up in the morning. Chasing things that aren't actually what you need will leave you feeling empty and unfulfilled, even if you manage to achieve them.

Being successful is directly linked to life satisfaction and genuine happiness. Isn't this everything that we want at the end of the day? We are all in the pursuit of being truly happy. For many of us, this is the elixir of life. It helps us find meaning, passion, and purpose. Whatever you define success to be is a unique and individual thing. There's no such thing as being too old to be successful. Worrying about age is often a crutch that we hang onto that prevents us from moving forward. It's an excellent excuse, but one that comes at one hell of a price.

Is the Timing Right?

You can't place a deadline on when you'll achieve success. However, what is certain is that the longer you postpone putting the wheels in motion, the longer you'll postpone becoming successful. What is certain is that only you will know when the time is right for you to clearly define your dream and then actively work toward achieving it.

Sometimes this timing isn't exactly right, and that's also okay. You must be committed to making your dreams become a reality. You may attempt something that you believe to be right at the time, only to fail. Instead of letting this failure paralyze you at that moment or prevent you from trying again, let it be a catalyst to keep going.

How will you know when the timing is right? First of all, you need to have a clear definition of what success means to you. It can't be someone else's dream for you—no matter how honorable the dream may be. You need to be able to own it, and the only way to do this is by identifying what will make you truly happy and fulfilled. What's going to give your life a sense of direction and purpose?

These may seem quite simple questions to have to ask yourself. In fact, they require deep reflection, and it may take a hell of a long time before you find the answers you're looking for. One of the things you should be aware of not doing is setting your goals because you've compared your current experiences to those of someone else. We've already discussed how toxic this can be.

Stop Comparing

Society is filled with these scenarios, and it's easy to get caught up in all the hype because they surround us. We're constantly comparing what we look like, what we do, where we live, and even who we've partnered with to those around us. Sometimes it's with people we don't even know. This behavior is toxic and something we need to get out of our system and stop doing. Working with comparisons, we don't even realize that we're looking at the surface exterior of someone's life that isn't even real, and we're trying to live up to this.

The beautiful images on Instagram, Facebook, or any other form of social media aren't a true reflection of the other person's life. Sure, there's nothing wrong with using these social media as a motivator, something to work toward in the future as long as you're not comparing yourself and where you're at on your life journey at the moment. The only thing you're likely to achieve is feeling more of a failure. What kind of motivator is this when it comes to determining your own success?

Please remember that even these people who seem to depict ultimate success and prosperity have their own set of challenges and obstacles. You know for yourself that life's not perfect. You have the first-hand experience with this. Don't for one moment think that the lives of those with picture-perfect social media images don't experience similar day-to-day challenges. You're not seeing or considering what has brought them to this point.

We don't think about trials and challenges that someone may have had to go through to get to where they are now. All that we see is the glossy end result, which we base our judgment on.

This isn't being realistic or honest with ourselves. Choosing to compare yourself against the rest of the world will only result in feeling insecure about yourself.

Once again, you're left chasing after the dreams of others rather than your own. To become who you are meant to become means being hard enough on yourself to see past all the smoke and mirrors that others present as their reality, recognizing where you have gotten to all on your own. You should be able to identify what you want based on your own value system.

For you to truly become successful in your life, you need to have a crystal-clear definition of precisely what success looks like to you and you alone. This means being able to visualize the end result. It means being able to dream about it to the point where you can describe it in every minute detail. When you close your eyes, you need to be able to see everything perfectly.

The Visualization Process

There are a couple of questions to ask yourself that will help you with your visualization process.

- What does success look like to me?

- What am I going to use to measure my performance?

- What will I feel like once I'm successful?

- Is my idea of success my own, or am I chasing someone else's dream?

- How do your values fit into your goals?

- Is this what you truly desire from life?

Spend enough time writing everything down. It's unnecessary to worry about what this looks like, even if you want to use other visual representations to perfectly capture each of these goals.

What's most important to you right now? How can you begin to prioritize some of these goals? The whole point of completing this exercise is to help you gain a better perspective as to where you are right now. It will also give you a better indication of where you need to go or what you need to do to get to where you want to be.

You can use what you have written down as both short- and long-term goals—being able to identify which of these will also help you break each of these down into smaller steps. You can only begin one small step at a time. This doesn't mean that your ultimate dream changes. All that it means is that you can identify many different milestones, smaller fragments of the ultimate goal that you can work toward.

Let's face it; if your goal was to climb Mount Everest, you certainly aren't going to begin in the middle (no matter how nice that might be.) You know that you're going to have to start at the bottom and work your way to the top. You need to be well-organized and prepared to face obstacles and challenges as they present themselves. Never really knowing where the next curveball is coming from.

This is what real life is like. We should know to expect the unexpected instead of hoping that everything in life will be perfect. Perfection is an unrealistic expectation. There will always be things that distract us and keep us from doing those things that are important. There will be challenges that we aren't expecting. Achieving your ultimate goal means moving forward steadily.

By starting small, you get a better idea of what working toward your ultimate goal is going to be like. If you find that you're not enjoying what you're doing, then maybe it's time to re-evaluate where it is that you want to go. What are you prepared to do to achieve your goal? The truth is that you should be willing to do whatever it takes. If you're not, then re-evaluation may also be necessary.

You're looking for things that are going to push you way out of your comfort zone. Things that are going to stretch you further than you've ever been before. They should also excite you enough to keep you motivated throughout the entire process. You want something that's going to help you want to keep going, even when times are tough. Times when you may be experiencing failure. It's important to understand that no failure is final. You shouldn't want to give up just because you hit a bit of a bump in the road. If anything, this should make you want to push even harder.

There have to be lessons from each of these experiences. If they're not blatantly obvious immediately, you may need to dig deeper to find them. Be prepared to put everything into your hopes and dreams for the future. If it doesn't require your blood, sweat, and tears, you may be left wondering whether it was all worth it, even when you achieve your goal. You should be feeling accomplished once you get there, rather than consistently working your butt off for something, and the end result isn't satisfying at all.

Chapter 2:

How the Hell did I Get Here?

I think we've each asked ourselves how the hell we got to where we are at some point in our lives. We analyze and overanalyze until it nearly drives us crazy trying to figure out what went wrong. Our focus is firmly fixed on everything that has happened in the past rather than where we're headed. When we do this, we risk living in the past, dwelling on situations and circumstances that we believe define us.

We're quick to blame where we are or aren't on those closest to us. Now, I'm not saying that your past cannot leave you screwed up because, more often than not, we have to wade through a lot of crap growing up; whoever told you that life would be easy lied!

I bet that one of the first words you learned was the word "NO." How do I know this? Well, that's pretty much what every parent will tell their toddler while trying to protect them. While parental intentions may initially be good, they don't realize they're setting up your default thought process. What I mean by this is that because we constantly hear that we shouldn't be doing certain things; eventually, we stop trying.

Regaining Your Identity

There are only so many times we can be told that we're stupid or useless before we begin to believe these things about ourselves. Unfortunately, it's usually those closest to us that influence the belief system we cling to for most of our lives. What our parents, peers, teachers, and other family members tell us can set us up either for failure or success.

You won't know which is which unless you sit back and question your current belief system. What is it that you believe about yourself deep down? Maybe you grew up as part of a dysfunctional family. You'll be forgiven for thinking everything was normal. It's when we're much older that we get to figure this out for ourselves. Maybe you survived a messy divorce where your parents were so focused on their issues they forgot you needed attention as well.

Maybe you were the victim of mental or emotional abuse because other kids bullied you at school. Feeling isolated at school often happens when you're slightly different from those around you. Thankfully you're only Looking back over your school or college life; hindsight is a beautiful thing. Once again, you may need to take a long hard look at where everything seemed to go pear-shaped for you. In many instances, it's not a single event that will have a negative impact on your life. It's an accumulation of things. In many instances, we don't even realize that what's holding us back is something that goes way back to our childhood. Instead, we blame all sorts of other things that may be happening in our lives at present. The real culprit is so deeply entrenched in our psyche that it may take serious introspection to get there.

Surviving physical or emotional abuse can be a bit trickier to deal with because the damage is permanent. Healing from these scars can take a lot of work. Abuse of any form is hard to block out as a coping mechanism is highly likely. You may even go through most of your life with fears and phobias you can't explain. In all honesty, this may take a lot of therapy and reliving most of these nightmares before you're able to face them head-on.

One of the biggest questions you need to ask yourself as you work through this process is whether you will allow any of these past situations to define who you are now. Don't let them hold you back from becoming the person you can become. The very first step is trying to fight your way through the fog that enshrouds your childhood.

As you try and remember each of the defining moments of your childhood, the chances are that you're going to come up with gaps. These gaps are where you need to focus your efforts. It's vital to try and put all the pieces of the puzzle that's your life back together again. It is best to work through these gaps with a counselor or therapist. Without working through the demons of your past, you'll keep circling back to the same point all over again. Until we learn how to deal with something and work through it, we'll continue to be haunted by it forever.

Quiet contemplation and serious soul-searching are often necessary to move past the limiting beliefs that are holding you back and preventing success. As long as you're prepared to give in to these experiences, you're giving them the power to determine your current and future success. Will you be able to dig your way out of past perceptions, or will they paralyze you in the present?

Where Do Limiting Beliefs Come From

What do you see when you look in the mirror? Are you still able to recognize the person looking back at you, or do you feel that somewhere along the way, you've lost your identity? It happens. Especially if you've had a shitty childhood, don't get me wrong, you can have the best parents in the world and still have a shitty childhood. Sometimes it's got nothing to do with your parents. You may come from a well-adjusted, loving home. A loving home doesn't mean that you'll always be protected from the big, bad world out there. This exposure may result in us creating a false persona or identity. Believing everything we've constantly been told may hamper our progress. It can stop us from even recognizing those things we want, let alone setting goals for ourselves and working toward them.

You may realize as you work through this process that it's other people in your life that have influenced how you feel about yourself. Regaining your identity especially after it's been molded by toxic people can take a whole lot of time, but it is possible. Relationships, even with those that are closest to you can prove to be messy. Because we're so close, we can't always see the damage that's being done. Usually, you only figure this out when it's too late.

Remember those gaps in your past recollections I was talking about earlier? The chances are that this was one of those times. Sometimes we identify with someone who's a failure or doesn't deserve the same success as those around us. Of course, this is complete BS, but the only person who can call you out on this is yourself. So maybe you weren't at the top of your class or had the honor of being prom king or queen. Perhaps you were a crappy cheerleader, or you never made the college football team.

Each of these things shouldn't be the reason why you no longer enjoy playing fair with the other kids in the sandbox of life. Maybe you're on the other side—where you feel that you're the one with none of the toys that every other big kid out there owns. No judgment here, but have you stopped to have a good look at how hard they've worked to get to where they are?

Sure, there will always be those born with a silver spoon in their mouths or get given everything on a silver platter. The key to your success is not stacking their lives up against your own. Doing so is only going to frustrate you further. The only person you need to compare yourself to is YOU. It's so easy to try and be someone that's way beyond your reach right now.

There's nothing wrong with having hopes and dreams for a better future. As a matter of fact, it's one of the first things you need to succeed. If you do not want to improve your current situation, you may need to dig deeper and reflect on yourself. I honestly don't believe you'll get to the point in your life when you can say you're 100% happy with who you are and what you've accomplished. Even once you've achieved your goals, you should have already set other goals that will stretch you even further.

Taking the Road Less Travelled

Can you identify who you are and visualize the path ahead that you've chosen for yourself? Is it a path you've chosen and one that will make you feel fulfilled and happy, or is it someone else's idea of where you ought to be heading? Are you doing what you want to do, or are you listening to what everyone else wants for you?

Maybe you feel you need permission from someone to live your life on your terms. Don't bother seeking validation from those around you. You may find that this is holding you back, preventing you from achieving the success you deserve. How can you change the perception you have of yourself? Can you do it alone, or do you need help? Accept that there's a distinct difference between needing support and needing validation or permission. Find those who are going to support you no matter what, without judgment.

Do you believe your future success is limited by or directly linked to past experiences? Believing this can keep you from attempting something that's out of your comfort zone. We don't need to be weakened by the things we've experienced in the past. We need to take responsibility for our lives instead of playing the blame game or using the past as an excuse for where we are now. Although it may be difficult, you can do it if you work through it the right way. If everyone chose to do this, we would be short visionaries who made lasting impressions on the world despite humble beginnings.

You've had a crappy past and can finally pinpoint where everything went wrong. How do you go about changing it? The first step is coming to terms with what has happened. Not always the easiest of things to work through, but you must be able to face these experiences to move beyond them. In doing so, you have one of two choices. You can choose to be a victim, or you can choose to be a survivor.

Choosing to be the victim may score you some points when it comes to throwing a pity party, but you'll battle to move past this. Once a victim, always a victim, or so this self-defeatist attitude would have you believe. It's easier to blame everyone else, especially your previous circumstances, for where you are or aren't currently. As long as you continue blaming others for your lack of success, you'll remain precisely where you are.

Maybe you're looking at those around you who all seem to have picture-perfect lives. Most of the time, this is merely just a façade. There is no such thing as the perfect background, the perfect upbringing, the perfect home, career, or life. Sure, this is something we'd all like to aspire toward, but perfection is subjective and open to interpretation. What I believe to be perfect may be far removed from your idea of perfection. In truth, there are only varying degrees of each of us doing our best. That's about as good as it's going to get.

What's Holding You Back?

Have you been able to identify what's holding you back? What's keeping you from living your very best life? What's keeping you from success, from joy, abundance, happiness, and yes, even wealth? Again, this takes time, effort, energy, and a hell of a lot of soul-searching. It's worth writing down whatever comes to mind, so you have something to expand on or refer back to.

Thinking long and hard about where you are now versus where you want to be will give you an idea of where you're falling short. Identifying what's holding you back gives you a springboard to work from to create the life of your dreams.

Are you wasting your time by bombarding yourself with endless questions? More time is wasted, focusing on the ifs, buts, what-ifs, could-haves, and should-haves, clouding your judgment and prevent you from living in the moment. What is it that you want from life? Try and clearly define your beliefs by putting them down on paper. By doing this, you'll eventually become so caught up in finding all the right answers that you lose sight of the end goal.

Stop comparing your life to the lives of others. It will end up driving you insane. There's only one of you, and that's the only person you should be worrying about when it comes to getting the best out of life. And no, this isn't adopting a selfish approach. Think about it for a moment. If you want to show up for anyone else, whether it's your friends, family, or loved ones, you need to show up for yourself first.

It's easy to assume that those who are successful in life have had it easy. Unless we've lived their lives or walked in their shoes, we don't know what they've had to do to become successful. We cannot begin to understand the road they've traveled to get to where they are. We don't know how many obstacles they've had to overcome or how many mistakes they've made along the way. Instead, we take a look at our lives and feel less than capable. We think we need to live up to unrealistic expectations. Can you see just how shortsighted, unreasonable, and limiting this thinking is?

Instead of worrying about everyone else, what are you doing about your journey? Are you spending all your time focusing on all the wrong things? It's easy to get caught up in all sorts of things that aren't productive. Sure, they keep you busy, but it's not the right kind of busy. It's taking your eye off the ball, and instead of focusing on the goalposts, you get completely distracted.

Chances are you've had a couple of those days when instead of getting things done, you end up doing everything that's unproductive. You know those days when you know you have deadlines to reach, and instead of getting stuck in, you just get stuck. You get caught up shuffling papers, spending hours on social media, or just staring into space searching for inspiration. It's easy to get caught up with distractions that will waste your time, something you can never get back again.

On the other hand, you may not want to waste another moment of your time because you want success, and you want it now! Unfortunately, life doesn't work that way. Expecting things to fall in your lap because that's what you want isn't realistic at all. Everything worth having in life takes time. In most instances, it takes a whole lot of blood, sweat, and tears as well. Time has a funny way of teaching us life lessons. It either teaches us patience or spurs us into action. You see, we either expect results to be instantaneous, or we're sitting waiting for the ideal moment before taking action.

Everything needs to happen as it should, and as they say, all good things come to those who wait—patiently. Okay, so maybe that's something you need to work on. We need to know when to practice patience and when it's time to get off our asses and do something about it. Sure, we live in an instant world where almost everything is at our disposal and right at our fingertips. Don't get caught up in the hype of quick fixes; get rich quick schemes and every other promise of instant success. As cliché as it may sound, the only place money comes before work is in the dictionary. Looking for the easy way out is not the answer. There's nothing wrong with wanting success, wealth, happiness, and everything that goes along with it.

Stick With It!

Do you believe you don't deserve success because you're just not talented enough? After all, everyone you know that's successful has a wall full of qualifications or years of experience. That's precisely my point. It's the experience you should be aiming for. The secret to success is wanting it bad enough that you're prepared to see it through no matter what. You need to be ready to stick with it no matter what.

As important as it is to stick with it, it's also wise to know when to quit. Not everything we touch will turn out to be a success just because that's what we want. There's wisdom in knowing when to give in and when to give up. Sometimes we cling to things for so long because we want them to work. Remember that not everything always goes according to plan. Letting go doesn't mean that you've failed and will never be successful—it just means that you're not meant to succeed in what you're currently doing.

You may be asking yourself, "why even bother if I'm not going to succeed?" Sure, you may not succeed the first time around or the second time around. All you need to do to figure out that this is a fact of life is to picture yourself learning many things in a concise space of time as a baby. You would never be able to walk had you not fallen a couple of times. You never gave in then, so why should you give in now.

Most of the successful people you admire have failed more than they've succeeded. Life is like that. Each failure inches you even closer to success. Every time you get knocked down, you need to be able to get up no matter what. Without this attitude, you'll always be wondering how the hell you got to where you are now.

Chapter 3:

Believing the Lies

Stop believing all the lies you've been told in the past that are holding you back.

Dreams of success should be what's motivating us to do something more with our lives. Let's face it; there will always be goals and dreams we want to achieve or manifest. Instead of doing something about these goals and dreams, we look for reasons we don't deserve health, wealth, happiness, and abundance. This toxic thinking is holding us back. All that we're doing is making excuses rather than taking action.

The chances are that you believe a whole host of lies you've been told in the past. These lies break down our self-esteem and self-confidence. Doubt and despair replace what should be hope for a brighter, more abundant future. It's easy finding reasons why you shouldn't bother pursuing your dreams. The main reason is that you believe the lies.

You're probably focused so much on worrying about everything that can go wrong instead of choosing to concentrate your efforts on chasing after your dreams. Finding excuses is perhaps one of the easiest things you can choose to do with your time. Making excuses is not going to bring you any closer to the life that you want. Instead, it's going to keep you from everything you've ever wanted. You'll end up trapped in the past or the present, too afraid to attempt anything.

The Toxic Lies We Tell Ourselves

It's easy for negative thoughts to take over what should be positive thinking. You should be looking at ways to live up to your potential instead of looking for reasons why you can't or won't put in the effort. Your thoughts are compelling. They can hold you back, or when they're positive, they can motivate you to work toward anything your heart desires. I can tell you which I would rather choose.

When you look back at the goals that are constantly just out of reach, you will probably find that somewhere in your thinking, you've convinced yourself that you'll never get there. That it's too hard, that you're probably going to give up halfway there. There are hundreds of excuses to be made. Believing in these lies is going to keep you from the life you deserve. So, what are some of these lies, and why do we think it's worthwhile mentally accepting that this is reality?

My Age is Against Me

I'm either too young or too old to see my goals and dreams become a reality. Sure, when you were younger, you may have had plans for a bright future. As we become older, the way we thought our lives would turn out may be completely different from our current reality.

Hey, when I was a teenager, I wanted to study law to become an advocate. I can't tell you how far removed from that dream my life is now. But that's precisely the point. We don't always get what we want. Our priorities and plans change. Life happens, and we need to deal with obstacles that we never even thought about when we were young.

Let's face it; this whole adulting thing is way different than we thought it would be. The point of worrying about your age will drive you crazy! You're not too young to start planning the life you want. Stop putting obstacles in the way that don't need to be there. Especially not when it comes to your age.

All that this will take to sort out is going back to identifying and accepting where you are now. You need to have this starting point and a clear line of sight on your goals. Without this, no matter how much effort you put in will be of any value to you whatsoever.

Stop thinking that your age is what's holding you back; this is utter BS. It's a limiting belief, and you need to recognize it as such to address it. Stop thinking you need someone else's permission or validation before you take action. Stop comparing where you are now to where you wanted to be, especially against those around you.

If others are holding you back, then it may be time for you to cut them loose. It's those kinds of relationships that are toxic. They do nothing to build you. Instead, they break you down even further. You have to believe in yourself. If you don't, then how can you expect anyone else to believe in you?

The Timing Just Isn't Right

The lie is that you believe you need to wait until you've done x, y, or z before you start working on your goal. The truth is that if you're waiting for everything to be perfect, nothing will ever happen. You will always have demands on your time, other things you need to do. There will always be places to go and people to meet. Such is life, and no number of excuses in the world will ever change the fact.

What can you do about your thought process? What's holding you back? Fear of failure? Fear of success? Fear of what other people might say? The problem with waiting for the right moment is that you end up wasting so much time—time you can never get back again.

Let's get back to your hopes and dreams. Do you know exactly what you want? The chances are that your goals and dreams aren't clearly defined. If you know what you want out of life and you have a plan in place. The cliché that time waits for no one is applicable here. If you know what you want, then what the hell are you waiting for? Get rid of the voices in your head that are only fueling your negativity. They're doing you no good.

Where does each of these beliefs come from? There will always be an excuse out there that you can latch onto instead of taking action. Maybe you need to check out your goals to be sure they are clear, it's what you want, and then figure out what you need to do to get there. Whatever you choose to do doesn't need to be anything huge. Small, constant action toward achieving your goals will at least keep you moving forward rather than stagnating or moving backward.

Believing You Don't Deserve to Achieve Your Goals

Hell no! If you can't believe in yourself, how do you expect anyone else to have faith and believe in you? Once again, this goes back to being afraid to succeed. Fear is like cancer that continues to grow. Remember that whatever you choose to believe in will become a reality. If you believe you're going to fail, then that's what's going to happen.

You're giving your thoughts the ability to not only control you but to control the outcome of your life. What's the point of that? Give yourself a break from all the negative thinking. There's enough of it out there already without you adding even more fuel to the fire. Once again, focus on finding what's making you believe that you don't deserve to achieve your goals.

Instead of giving in to fear and doubt, try and figure out whether there's something that you need to do differently and then do it. Re-examine your thinking. Focus on your attitude toward success and achievement. If you don't believe you can, no amount of wishing will turn your doubts into success. It all goes back to what you believe in.

Shift your thinking toward success. Take the first step by actually deciding that you're worthy of your goals. Once you've been able to solidify this belief, you can take the next step toward everything you've ever wanted—get off your ass and do something about it. Even if you're afraid that you're going to fail, replace this belief with one where you recognize that doing something toward reaching your goals and failing is better than doing nothing.

Success Is Meant for Others

This lie is one where you think that everyone else has so much more than you, and they deserve it, while you're where you're meant to be. If this is what you keep telling yourself, then that's what will happen, and others will always have more than you. Stop pitching yourself against everyone else. Your life is yours and yours alone. Stop comparing and complaining. It's almost as if you're looking for a scapegoat when you do.

Come to terms with the fact that even when you become successful, there will always be someone better than you, someone, who has more than you have, and it shouldn't bother you in the slightest. As long as you are content within yourself, why should anyone else's success be making any difference to your own life? The more time we waste comparing ourselves to others, the more we take the eye off our own ball. We stop thinking about all the things we want because we'd rather have what others have.

Our goals need to be as unique to ourselves as our fingerprints and DNA are. The problem with becoming engrossed with the success of others is that you don't see what's going on behind the scenes. Everything looks so perfect and wonderful when it really isn't. They have the same challenges that you have, if not even more. Stop feeling that those around you are better than you. All that this is doing is making you feel bad about yourself.

If you're battling with this problem, then it may be time to unplug for a while. Look for the lies and limiting beliefs that you're handing your power to. Recognize each of these lies for what they are and the damage they're doing by keeping you from living the life that you deserve. Not the life of someone else—your goals and thinking need to realign with who you are. You need to focus on your success and all the reasons why you deserve to be successful. Whatever you focus on long enough will become your reality.

Success Isn't Possible

There's no such thing as impossible. This thinking is skewed. It will get you to believe that because something looks difficult, it's automatically unattainable. If we had to turn away from everything difficult, challenging, or uncomfortable, then we may as well stop living. Any success we achieve is going to take work to get there. If you believe you can't get there, you won't. It's part of the Law of Attraction. Whatever we put out there is what we'll experience. Stop setting yourself up for failure. Don't you deserve way more than this?

I'm Going to Fail

So what if you fail. Anyone who has achieved any measure of success in their lives will be the first to tell you how many times they failed before they succeeded. Failure and success go hand in hand. The lie is that getting what you want out of life is something that's automatically going to happen-life will be plain sailing without experiencing anything negative. It is simply not true.

Before you can learn and grow, you need to fall down a couple of times. The more you fail, the more you'll learn. Imagine all the experience you can gain along the way. However, you'll only be able to make the changes you need to when you can identify where you've gone wrong. Also, be careful what you tell yourself internally every time you do fail. For instance, if you're telling yourself that everything's a failure, then, of course, everything will be a failure. Start thinking positively for once.

Nobody Cares if I Succeed or Fail

You're probably right, but if you're going to wait until someone notices that you're successful, you'll be waiting a long time. Why are you so caught up in wanting validation from other people? This type of validation is something that you were taught as a child. Your parents needed to give you permission. When you were at school, it was your teachers, at college, your professors. When you started working for the first time, you had a manager or business owner that told you what you could or couldn't do.

Okay, so I get it. But the point is, when will you realize that the only person you need validation from is yourself. Instead of worrying about others noticing your success. You're past the stage of needing a pat on the back and an "atta boy!" Believing this lie is juvenile.

Set Your Standard and Raise the Bar

Choose to surround yourself with those you know will be in your corner when you need them to be; this will probably be your family members and your closest friends, but that's okay. Choose to associate with those who give a damn about what happens to you. Relationships may be meaningful, but your connection with total strangers can hold you back. Worry about how your success is going to make you feel instead. It will prevent you from experiencing what success and achievement feel like.

Limiting beliefs are just another set of lies that we believe. These are the stories we tell ourselves that we believe to be true and keeps you focusing on all the small, inconsequential things. Rather than doing the things that aren't going to get you anywhere, ask yourself what will make you feel better about yourself? What's going to give you a sense of satisfaction and fulfillment?

Limiting beliefs stem from our childhood. These come from all the times we were told we weren't good enough, smart enough, talented enough. It comes from being told that we were useless, stupid, irritating, etc., this list can go on and on, but I think you get the point.

Believing these things can be extremely destructive. Deep down, we know that none of these things are true, but we give them power over us because we believe them. We allow these beliefs to determine whether we're going to succeed or fail. They can either build us up or break us down. Only we hold power to be able to change the way we respond to any of these beliefs.

We should be taking responsibility for whether or not we achieve success. Instead, we stop believing in ourselves, or the only self-beliefs we have are limiting. We let all these lies dictate the action we take. It's time to accept that you're the only one holding yourself back. Instead of simply accepting whatever is going through your head, stop and ask yourself whether your thinking is genuine. Can you provide proof to back up your belief? If not, then it's time to let your thinking go.

Far too often, we look to blame someone else for what's happening in our lives. After all, it's their fault we're not successful. Get to the point where you regain control of your life. Make your own choices and decisions, rather than allowing anyone to dictate what happens to you. It's unhealthy living in the past, where you're still trapped in the body of your younger self.

If you're still not sure whether the things floating around in your head are real or not, it's worth finding someone to talk to. You may even be able to distinctly recall every negative, berating comment ever made to you. That's fine. It's healthy when you're trying to move beyond living in the past. Choose to focus on and live in the moment. It's the only way for you to be able to discover and live your truth, rather than someone else's truth.

Find someone you like and trust, but someone who isn't going to sugarcoat anything for you. You want someone who's going to call you out when your thinking is all screwed up. It would help if you had someone who will be honest with you. This type of support is one of the few ways to find out what you need to change about your behavior and backing this up with action.

Finally, when it comes to the lies you believe, the only person you should be worried about is yourself. We've spoken about stacking yourself up against others. Instead of doing this, why not raise the bar for yourself, against yourself. What can you do now to make the difference between where you are now and where you want to be? Even if it's something small that you do every single day. Each of these small things can eventually become one big thing.

It's like putting a small snowball together on the top of a snow-filled slope and sending it on its way. That snowball can eventually turn into an avalanche with the right intention behind it. Get past all the lies you've been feeding yourself since you were younger. You need to regain control of your life. Get back into the drivers' seat, rather than being content with playing passenger and going along for the ride.

If you've been sitting back, waiting for things to come your way simply, then it's time to wake up; this isn't how the world works.

You need to be prepared to do everything in your power to reach your goals. You will need a firm commitment with yourself that you're prepared to do whatever it takes to get there. It doesn't matter if you fail a couple of times. Remember that all successful individuals, even those famous entrepreneurs you admire for their confidence, have had to start somewhere. They've also failed way more often than they've succeeded. The difference between them and us is that we take failure personally instead of leveraging the lessons learned, turning failure into success.

Stop stressing about impressing anyone else out there. The only person you should be worried about is yourself, your success, your goals, hopes, dreams, and the achievement of all of the above. Don't lose faith or hope because you're living in the past. You have the power to be able to change your belief system.

You have the power to be able to raise the bar. You are the only one you should be comparing yourself to. You are the only one who can stop believing the lies from your past. The reason for this is that you're the one who began to believe these lives in the first place. Just like that snowball, you've turned these lies into something bigger than they needed to be.

You can analyze where they come from and be realistic regarding whether they have merit or not. Remember that there's no such thing as being too young or too old for success. There's no such thing as not being worthy of success or others being more deserving than yourself. Moving beyond this point may not be the easiest thing that you've ever done, but it will all be worth it in the end.

Chapter 4:

Dealing With the BS

If you're anything like me, chances are you keep asking yourself how you got to the point where you've surrounded yourself with so much BS. It would be great to have a neat and tidy life with everything wrapped in a bow, but that isn't real. As cliché as it may sound, we all go through life with rose-tinted glasses on at some stage or another. Skimming through magazines, we all wish that our lives were somehow different and that if they were, then we'll finally be happy.

Our benchmark is nothing short of perfection. Let's face it; we know realistically that no amount of effort will bring us close to the perfection we expect to achieve. Perfection is unattainable because the moment we set the stakes this high, we're setting ourselves up for failure. It's not so much whether we have to deal with a mountain of crap at any given time. It's how we handle it that counts.

Become Accountable for the BS

What does your life look like at the moment? Are there parts of it that you're not happy with? If you've answered yes to this question, then welcome to the human race. We all have this in common. Suppose we didn't, then there would be something seriously wrong with us. There will always be something we wish we had a better handle on.

Figuring out where to start can be overwhelming. Let's face it when there's so much happening, even pinpointing what needs work will prove almost impossible. Do you concentrate your efforts on real stuff like your home, or do you need to work on things that hold deeper meaning, like your health and wellbeing? How about your relationships, your work, your financial situation?

Have you considered the possibility that you are the one responsible for the way things are in your life right now? One of the most significant challenges we face is coming to terms with all the crap in our lives. It's easy to blame everyone for where we find ourselves other than taking a look in the mirror. That's right—The only person responsible for getting us to where we are right now is ourselves.

The time has come for you to hold yourself accountable for whatever happens in your life. Accountability means you realize that you and you alone are responsible for everything that happens to you. Accountability helps you become more focused on your goals or those things you'd like to achieve. Whether this means having to face the facts honestly or avoiding procrastination there are many other positive results to be enjoyed.

Being accountable means because you know you're responsible for your destiny when things go wrong, you understand who's to blame. You don't look for scapegoats or excuses. Instead, you face up to cold hard facts that aren't always easy to swallow. You come to grips with how self-sabotage can prevent you from succeeding. You understand exactly what role fear plays in all of this. At the same time, you know that fear is just another obstacle you need to move beyond to succeed.

Becoming accountable for our own lives doesn't happen overnight. None of us want to admit we've messed up. After all, admitting to mistakes can be seen as a sign of weakness. If we're thinking, then how is this belief holding you back? There's a big difference between allowing things to happen to you and taking responsibility for what does happen.

The first behavior is choosing passive resignation rather than being proactive. How do you know which way you are leaning? Are you happy to go with the flow and live in the moment or have you figured out that nothing is going to change unless you do?

As with most things in life that need to be changed or worked on, we should first identify what's holding us back. What are we doing now that is limiting our progress? For this to be effective, we need to question our motives.

Are these motives still closely aligned, moving in the same direction as our ultimate goals? Maybe we have veered so far. Of course, it's going to take some serious sweat equity getting back. The truth is that you won't know unless you closely analyze where you are now against where you want to be.

See Through the BS

Ask yourself what's holding you back? Chances are it's a big fat excuse. Time to uncover it, write it down, and examine it. You will no doubt find way more than just one thing. Write each of these down as a way to see what you should do to change. If you're realistic about it, you'll know that you can only try and change a couple of things simultaneously rather than doing everything at once.

Are there things you need to let go of? It's time to realize that you can't control everything in life. There will always be a whole host of things beyond your control. We fall short when we try to change things we have no power over. It means being realistic about what is happening around us.

By writing things down, it becomes easier to identify what we're dealing with. How much of this can we control, and how much do we need to let go. When you do this exercise, you likely recognize that you can't control everything around you.

The cold hard truth is that none of us can go through life without any problems. Sure, it would be great if this were true. I think we each wish we had that silver bullet, the magic potion pixie dust, or whatever. Stop living in a pipe dream. There's no such thing other than in fairy tales, and chances are our lives are more like a nightmare.

We are wasting our time looking at everything wrong with our lives when we should focus on how we deal with these hiccups or inconveniences. And that's what these are; they're merely obstacles standing directly between us and where we want to be. Wanting to live a life without challenges or obstacles is an unreasonable expectation.

It's not the size of the challenge or obstacle that stares us down. It's what we do with these barriers that is important. We can either shrink back into our lives, resigned to the fact that we are facing something much bigger than us, or we can try and do something about it. No matter the size of the challenge, as we make an effort to work through it, there will be individual life lessons vital to our progress.

There's no such thing as the perfect life, the perfect marriage, the perfect kids, the perfect career. There are only the cards we've been dealt. Sure, they might not always be fair, but nothing in life is ever that clean cut. We may not like where we are on this journey. Maybe it's uncomfortable or too challenging for us right now. That's okay. Work through what you can and leave what you can't.

Get with the program when it comes to how the level of crap you're trying to wade through is keeping you from living the life you want. There's no way you can manifest abundance when you're so fixated on everything wrong. If you don't know by now that whatever you spend all your time thinking about is what is currently manifesting in your life, chances are you never will.

Accept That Life Is Messy

Re-examine your belief system. Is this belief system affecting your life when it comes to negative thinking? This is part of the problem rather than the solution. To understand where negative thinking comes from, you may need to return to those earlier experiences you had as a child. Is there something there that's causing you to believe the things you do about yourself? Can you validate your thinking by finding proof that what you believe is true?

It's not so much what goes into our minds as it is what we give power to. Not all of our thoughts are good for us. Most of them can be destructive. The world has us comparing ourselves against an impossible set of standards. It's up to us to sift through these beliefs to identify what's valid and what should be ignored.

You cannot go through life without problems. If this were the case, then none of us would grow. We'd choose to limit ourselves when it comes to learning through experience. Growth is only possible when we're prepared to go through the pain that accompanies change. Without change, we're stagnating. Without change, we're telling ourselves that we're happy with where we are.

If you've identified what's holding you back and you're not prepared to do anything about it, then it's unrealistic to expect further progress. What you believe has a positive or negative effect on how you think and how you act. It doesn't mean that what you believe is accurate.

Getting back to when you formed these belief systems, you need to cast your mind back to when you were much younger. Many beliefs have resulted from things we were told, experiences we had, and even the experiences of others. The only way to counteract the destructive influence that these beliefs have is to challenge them. The truth is that there are a whole lot of factors that determine our beliefs. It's not just a single thing.

We often need to be told something repeatedly before we get to the point of believing it. If someone had to pass a comment that you don't look well, you'd probably shrug it off and carry on with your day. Whereas if everyone you happen to come across all tells you the same thing, guaranteed you'll be on the phone making a doctor's appointment. You may even present with physical and psychosomatic symptoms. They're not real, but you now have a firm conviction that it has to be true if everyone says so. Just like when we were younger, this is an example of precisely what happens. Chances are several people told us the same thing over an extended period. Our beliefs can be damaging to our entire future unless we get them under control. The first step is pulling every negative belief we have about ourselves apart. If you cannot find solid proof that what you've been believing is true, you can likely change your core belief.

Get Over the Drama of Toxic People

Is all the BS surrounding you making you cynical in your outlook toward life? Understand that the world is full of toxic people who would like nothing more than to see you fail. Developing meaningful relationships with these individuals will be draining because they're so full of negativity that they sap all the energy out of you. All they can see is doom and gloom, and because that's how they live their lives, they want everyone around them to be the same. They're not happy unless you're wading through the crap with them.

You may be in denial, believing that you're positive and everyone around you has a problem. Maybe that's true, but the more time you spend with those who are negative and would like nothing more than to see your ass fail, the greater chance you have of failing. That's the problem with toxic people. Their negativity rubs off like the plague. They are destructive and thrive on the misfortune of everyone around them.

It may be time for you to reassess the relationships you have with those around you. Ask yourself the tough questions that aren't always comfortable. Is your relationship moving you closer to your goals or farther away from them? You'll be able to tell this by listening to your inner dialogue whenever you're in their company. Also, stop and listen to what they're saying and how this makes you feel.

Once you've confirmed that a relationship is toxic, it may be time to cut the cord. It won't always be possible, depending on the actual relationship. Some relationships can't simply be disregarded. If it happens to be a family member, you obviously can't simply cut ties with them. Try to minimize your exposure to constant negativity by limiting the amount of time spent in their company.

It's worth mentioning that you need to come to terms with the fact that not everyone can be upbeat. There are way more negative people out there than positive ones. It's a direct result of the world we live in. Think about how our exposure to television, online content, and the media influences our perception of the world. Let's face it most of this content is negative because that's what sells. You'll seldom find anything that will give you the warm fuzzies in most online material.

All this negativity carries through into your life and influences your future success or failure. Instead of allowing negativity to alter the trajectory of where you want to be, it may be time to toughen up to the point where you can disregard it. Your main aim is to get past believing anything negative about yourself. Even if you may have been like that in the past, you need to pull out all the stops when deciding your beliefs; this means being able to tell what's negative from what's neutral or positive. All you need to ask yourself is whether it makes you feel better about yourself or worse. If you think that you're worse off, then it's time to let the relationship go. Part of dealing with toxic people is moving past them without giving them the power to disrupt your life.

Taking the Next Steps

What if you happen to have made your own crap? To be honest, you're going to have to work through it so you can eventually get through it. That's not to say that dealing with it is going to be easy. Of course, it depends on the amount of BS you're trying to wade through.

One of the essential parts of dealing with it is owning it. Admit to the fact that you have a problem. It's once you own up to it that you can begin to make any changes necessary. Facing up to it is the first step in the right direction. You will need to do everything in your power to break the cycle. Meaning you need to be completely in the driver's seat when it comes to your life, where you're going, and how you're planning on getting there.

Don't be too proud or afraid to ask for help from those you trust. Too often, we convince ourselves that to be successful or work through problems, we need to work through everything independently; this is not true. This is one of those lies that we were told when we were younger. If you believe this, then the chances are that you were told to "suck it up, tough it out, face it like a grown-up," or anything else along the same lines. No matter how tough an exterior you may have. There will always be a need for human contact and interaction. That's part of being human. We desperately need that companionship. We crave approval from others for some reason before looking inward.

We know we need to prove something to those around us, but we feel we have to do it all independently and won't admit we need help. It's time for you to get over yourself. Cut the crap and accept the help from those who are older, wiser, or have way more experience than you. We allow ourselves to be so stubborn that it sets us back when it comes to reaching our goals or achieving success.

Have you heard the cliché about the grass being greener on the other side of the fence? Because of all the shit that lies there, that's what happens with life. We want everything to be smooth sailing. Instead, things are pretty messy. Life's messy, our relationships are messy, working toward our goals is messy. An entire range of things can be mentioned here that would all fall under the "messy category."

We look at the lives of others, and most of the time, we'll gladly exchange what we believe to be an imperfect life for one that's seemingly perfect. In truth, there's no such thing as the perfect life. The rosier things appear from the outside. You need to know that there's way more there than meets the eye. It's only when you fully understand the full story that you can begin to appreciate things as they are rather than the way you want them to be.

Through the chaos and the mess, a sense of order can come when we handle it correctly. The most important steps to take include deep introspection to identify any red flags that could point toward all the things going on inside your head. Assess each of these beliefs to determine whether they're valid or whether they belong to someone else.

Make a judgment call but one in the best interest of your goals and future dreams. Don't expect anyone else to assume responsibility for what happens in your life. It's your responsibility. Own it and move forward with confidence rather than fear.

Chapter 5:

Taking Names and Kicking Ass

There are so many ways that negativity has a direct influence on our lives. Think about how many times you give focus on everything that can go wrong in a situation. Your brain automatically defaults to negativity. Instead of looking for the good, we're wired to concentrate on the bad. We've already spoken about the way that bad news sells. We get off on hearing about the massive cash heist or how many people were arrested after a random shooting.

How many times do you get bogged down by the mistakes you make in life? You play situations over and over again in your mind. You're searching for all those things you did wrong. You don't look for what went right. There's much more weight given to the negative rather than the positive. When we are criticized by someone, especially someone we like, trust, or admire, it holds way more power than a compliment.

Negativity also holds much more power. We automatically go there, and it directly influences our reaction to the situation. It can control the way we think and the way we act. It has the power to affect relationships on all levels negatively. We have close relationships with those we love and relationships we have with those we work with, friends, family, and even those we interact with.

When something negative happens, we remember everything about it, but we replay these things repeatedly in our minds. Explaining why all the bad stuff from our past can't be left there. We have no problem being able to recall the events down to every last gory detail.

How Our Past Beliefs Affect Us Now

Past trauma can influence our lives in the present more than all the good times we may have experienced. We overreact more when we receive bad news than when we receive good news. The bad will always overshadow the good. This focus on all the bad things that have already happened or possibly can happen can influence our lives.

Psychologically it's much easier for us to find more reasons why we shouldn't be doing something rather than why we should. We often don't do something because we've already decided that something terrible is going to happen. We bring this negative thinking into the mix instead of looking at the good that can come out of it. It's almost like we give up rather than finding ways to succeed. It is only different when we're scared and we don't want to lose something.

So, how do negative thinking and negative behavior affect our lives?

We stop trying to achieve our goals because we feel that there's no point in even trying. Instead, we're prepared to sacrifice anything good that can come from giving it our all. You don't bother doing whatever it takes to get to where you want to be. It becomes easier to lose your temper over trivial things instead of looking for reasons to be cheerful. We stay upset a lot longer than necessary. All it takes is for something small that's negative to happen to us when we're having a great day. We lose our shit and stay in a bad mood for the rest of the day.

Think about times when you've had a disagreement or argument with someone you care about. Chances are you spend too much time focused on the hurtful things that were said rather than thinking about all the good times you've had. It's because of this behavior that relationships fail. Instead of being able to move past the small things, we'd rather focus on them. We expect others to disappoint us.

We expect to fail instead of being able to succeed. Expecting to fail is one of the ways that negativity keeps us from manifesting abundance in our lives. We constantly think about why we won't succeed rather than why we can. We look for everything that's going to keep us from achieving everything that we deserve. That's part of the problem because we don't believe that anything good should happen to us. They say that this kind of thinking originated from our ancestors as a way to keep them safe. It makes sense that this mechanism is built into who we are at the very core. It's not to say that it's okay to use this as an excuse for not getting to where you want to be. It's not okay to hang onto this negativity as an excuse for how you treat those around you. How you treat your goals or your motivation to do whatever it takes.

The Power of Negativity

Negative thinking affects our mental health. It makes perfect sense when you think about how you fixate on the bad rather than the good. Our thought process is skewed. Realistically we know that there are a lot of good things out there. We need to look for them. We can't do this when all we see are the things that will hold us back. We battle to be optimistic about the future.

How much of this negativity is happening in your head? Chances are almost all of it. That's where all the replay happens. When do we stop and question the way we're thinking? Are there things you could have learned from your mistakes instead of only thinking you messed up? Try and focus on the lessons instead of what you may have done wrong. If you can learn from what happened, you don't need to keep going back to doing the same thing repeatedly.

Are you viewing yourself in a negative light? If yes, this will influence whether you succeed or continue to fail. Not everything in life is negative. If we think this way, then we're setting ourselves up for a miserable life. There has to be something positive at the other end of the scale for a negative to exist. It's able to recognize the good for what it is.

Stop and analyze how you're thinking and reacting toward situations as they happen in your life. Challenge what you're thinking and how you're interpreting these situations. You'll quickly be able to recognize that your thinking is negative if everything you believe is bad. It's time to realize that there are always two sides to a coin. Both the good and the bad are connected and always will be. By looking hard enough, you'll be able to see that there's just as much good out there. Sure, it may be challenging to shift your thinking. You may need to actively work on it before it becomes a habit.

Instead of automatically defaulting to the negative subconsciously, choose to look for the good. To do this means looking for ways to break your current thought pattern by doing something else. Deciding to do something different, something that will make you happy, can change your outlook on life. Pay attention when you have a positive experience. Yes, your brain will automatically try and focus on everything wrong. If you know that the chances of this happening are pretty great, then you can do something about it.

Remember that you have a choice when it comes to what you believe. We have a choice about everything in life. You choose to believe that things in your past are the reason for not succeeding in the future. You have a choice as to whether you are going to bring your past baggage with you. Making this decision can lead to physical stress and anxiety.

We become what we believe; this translates into whether we think we are capable or not. Whether we believe we deserve a better life or whether we believe we ought to be stuck in the same old rut we've been in. What we believe is extremely powerful, and whenever we give in to what society dictates, we're handing that power over to someone else. It's giving up rather than making any effort to break through this mold of mediocrity.

Ultimately it still boils down to a choice. Consciously you may need to change what you keep telling yourself. Question where your thoughts are coming from. Question what's driving the thoughts and emotions you have toward success. What's making you believe that you're not worthy? Are you trying to work through previous experiences, or are you scared of success? What's your strongest motivation at the moment?

Overcome Negative Thinking

Some of the ways we can try and overcome negative thinking is by watching what's going into our minds. What are we paying attention to? Are we fixated on how bad things are or can we still manage to find the good in a bad situation? Sure, this isn't going to be easy, but then again, nothing in life that's worth having is going to come easily.

One of the ways we can try and overcome negative thinking is by watching what's going into our minds. What are we paying attention to? Are we fixated on how bad things are, or can we still manage to find the good in a bad situation? Sure, this isn't going to be easy, but then again, nothing in life that's worth having is going to come easily.

They say you become like the people you associate with. Think back to the toxic relationships we discussed in the previous chapter. Most of these individuals are driven by making others as miserable as they are. They don't want us to do better than them. They're happy to see you fail rather than succeed. These are the relationships you need to question. Are these the type of people you enjoy being with? Are they building you up or breaking you down? Chances are it's the latter. We also become like the people we choose to associate with. Look for those around you that are positive. You may need to let them give you the odd lecture on changing the way you are thinking. Maybe this will shake you enough to pay closer attention to your thought patterns.

Try and replicate this by associating with those that are more positive than negative. It's amazing how we become like those we choose to associate with. Switch out the toxic and grab onto the lifeline that positive individuals can offer. They're probably much happier than you are when you choose to wallow in misery. Stop and assess who you're spending the most time with. Those people may not be the right fit for you, especially if they're helping you fuel your negativity. You know, the type who constantly whines about everything. They even complain about things they have no control over; this is wholly counterproductive and adds to your already unhealthy negativity.

The Positive People in Your Life

There's a difference between those that are detrimental to your health and those that will help move you forward. Those close to you don't need to be excellent in everything they do, and they don't need to be a cut above the rest when it comes to having money. Their most important attribute will be their ability to shift your negative thinking. They'll be able to motivate you to snap out of it. Maybe it comes in the form of a challenge. Perhaps they'll encourage you to take action where you're currently marking time. They're probably happy with where they are—much more content than you are now, at least.

The positive people in your life are focused on seeing you succeed rather than fail. They'll encourage you to stretch yourself or push yourself farther. These are the people that will lift you when you're down rather than making you feel worse. They're going to call you out whenever you're looking for sympathy. I'm not saying that they're perfect. They've just learned that focusing on the good and being happy is better than focusing on the bad.

If you're still unsure who you're spending most of your time with, think about how you feel whenever you're with them. What's their overall attitude toward life? Do they make you feel better about yourself, or worse? Just like you and I, they're also trying to deal with all the drama that comes with everyday living. There's nothing different about them other than their attitude toward life and success.

They've learned what it takes to get out of the quagmire of mediocrity. They know that change is possible and that there's a direct link between happiness and success. Do you want to change how you think and how you behave? Then it's time to change your circle of influence. It's time to change the crowd you hang around with. It's time to let go of those that keep you stuck where you are now.

Reclaim Your Power

It's not easy to suddenly change overnight. Any form of change takes time. It would help if you were both realistic and kind to yourself. You are unique as an individual, and so are the people around you. Remember that what's important to you may not be important to them and vice versa. If you want things to change in your life, you also need to be prepared to make these changes. Do you know where you want to be?

Have you been able to identify what you want out of life? If not, then how can you ever expect to get there? There are a couple of questions you could be asking yourself to come up with the answers to. It's not like you're suddenly going to wake up with an epiphany that your life should be moving in a specific direction. It takes quite a lot of thought.

Stop and think about what's going to make you feel fulfilled? When you find this, you'll be able to discover what your primary motivation in life is. Why is this so important? If you're working toward things that aren't moving you closer to where you want to be, then chances are you'll lose interest. It's easy to give up something you don't enjoy rather than something that makes you happy. Once you know what this is, you'll be more inclined to keep doing more.

Being able to identify these things may take some deep introspection. Ask yourself what you love. What would you be prepared to do even if you weren't paid to do it? Are you doing what you're currently doing because you're living up to someone else's expectations of you? There's no way that this will bring you happiness or make you feel fulfilled—quite the opposite. If you're doing things to please other people, then you'll have a lot more regrets rather than feeling like you've done something worthwhile with your life. Essentially you're busy placing the needs of others before your own needs.

Trying to do what you believe you're expected to isn't living your own life at all. If you realize that this is what you're doing, there's no time to make the change. This is why knowing what's important to you is so vital. We've been programmed to think about others, putting them first in all that we do. When it comes to your life and what's best for you, only you can answer. You need to be prepared to become selfish about what you're doing and for who.

If you currently feel like you regret doing things in life, it may mean it's time for a change. It may be a sign that you're living in the past. Living in the past may mean you're giving in to the limiting beliefs that others have about you. Living your life purely for the sake of others will frustrate you, and chances are you'll end up living with a whole lot of regrets. You can't keep on living like this and achieve success. It's time to put the past behind you and pay more attention to what's happening right now. It's time to keep your sights on the future. Where are you going now, and what's going to help you move forward. Are you part of the problem, or can you find the solution?

What often happens is we don't believe that we deserve to be successful. We don't deserve to be happy, or we don't think we deserve the rewards attached to our goals. These beliefs are damaging and will keep us in the past. We need to stop paying attention to these thoughts and look at what we've already accomplished.

When have we been happiest? Were there any factors that contributed toward this that you can duplicate? Once again, you may need to spend some quiet time focused on identifying each of these things. You may be holding onto the belief that you should have succeeded long ago. You blame yourself for where you are now, passing harsh judgment toward actions you may or may not have taken. It's time to learn to let this go. The reality is that we are our own worst enemies. We blame ourselves for things that are often out of our control. Where introspection is healthy, blaming ourselves for things that have happened in the past will keep us stuck there.

It's easier to forgive others for their faults than to forgive ourselves. Rather than learning to let go, we keep on harping on the same old thing. We rehash choices that we've made, constantly questioning our motives. Isn't it time to learn to let things go? Isn't it time to take control of your life rather than have it control you?

If they can do it, then why can't we? Part of being able to forgive ourselves is admitting to what we've done wrong. It's making a conscious decision to try and learn from your mistakes rather than repeating them; this doesn't mean that we have to be perfect. Being aware of what's possibly triggered your actions, then you have something to work with. For this to become effective, you need to be able to let go. It's time to own your mistakes but recognizes that you aren't your mistakes. You're way more than that. It's time to take back the power to be able to live your life without regrets. Reclaiming your power is one of the few ways that you'll be able to put the past behind you and get to where you want to be.

Chapter 6:

Facing Fear

The nervous knot in the pit of your stomach or suddenly feeling that you need to quickly respond to a dangerous situation all come from fear. You're driving quite happily when all of a sudden, the car in front of you swerves and screeches as the driver brakes. Up ahead, there's a major collision. If you don't do something immediately, chances are you'll be joining the pileup. You hit your brakes as hard as you can, leaving half of your tire tread on the tarmac.

Within seconds your heart is racing, your palms are sweaty, your pupils have dilated, you suddenly have supersonic hearing. In the time it took you to react to what was happening in front of you, you could keep everything together. Before you reacted the way you did, you could assess the situation, check all your mirrors to see what was behind you and to each side of you. You knew that although you calculated your move, it would provide you with the best outcome. All you had to do was pray that the drivers behind you were alert enough to react in the same way.

This example is typical of a reaction to fear where imminent danger threatens your life. Of course, this isn't the only kind of response or type of danger out there, but chances are you can relate to what I'm talking about. Fear is an emotional reaction not only to threats that are there but also to things we believe will harm us. Many of these are perceptions. It's how we look at things mentally. This is where panic attacks and posttraumatic stress come in. They're psychological but cause genuine emotional distress.

Emotional stress is not always all bad when you're talking about how you feel jumping out of an aircraft (with a parachute, of course). There's going to be one hell of an adrenaline rush, probably until that parachute opens, Maybe even longer than that if you're not sure where you're going to land safely. A surge of adrenaline is like a drug. That's what keeps you getting back into a plane, ready to do it all over again. You're probably labeled as an adrenaline junkie. Now, this situation would be way different if you were afraid of heights. Chances are you'd be frozen in that aircraft, unable to move even if someone threatened to push you out. You're not driven by an adrenaline high here. High is the last place you want to be.

Some of the physical symptoms may be the same for everyone, but fear affects us differently. It's not always going to be a sweaty palm scenario. Maybe you feel like you have an elephant on your chest, and you're battling to breathe. Your nerves kick in, and you can't stop shaking. You're in a hot and cold sweat and feel nauseous.

How about that presentation you need to give to a room full of board members, and you are uncomfortable speaking in front of groups of people? This situation might leave you feeling totally out of control or overwhelmed by the situation. Maybe you're paralyzed in the moment. Your mouth is dry, and your thoughts are incoherent. You know you've got to get out there and fast.

Face up to Your Fears

They say that the best way to conquer fear is by facing it. Even if you're forced to deal with public speaking, it doesn't mean that these fears will automatically go away immediately. Sure, you may learn some coping mechanisms such as breathing exercises to help you initially.

Regularly facing your fears is the only way to reduce some of the adverse effects caused by fear. This example would mean getting used to speaking in front of people by taking every opportunity to practice. Make yourself available to give the same presentation regularly. Sure, you may feel like you're about to die for the first couple of attempts. Gradually you'll begin to feel more comfortable. So, what happens when you ignore these emotions? They're not going to get better or disappear on their own. Without minimizing the real effects of fear, chances started as fear can turn into panic. If you've ever felt afraid of being afraid, then you know what anxiety feels like.

Fearful emotions run high because we're programmed to look for the worst possible outcome. Doom and gloom are promoted through various media channels, keeping us from moving forward with our lives, holding us captive, or stuck where we are. We're too scared to do anything else, just in case. There is a hell of many ifs and buts here, yet we give them enough power to immobilize us.

Fear can keep us stuck in the past or the present when it comes to manifesting abundance and making the most of our lives. Because we're afraid to take risks, to possibly fail a couple of times, we don't even bother to try. We're afraid of failure; we're afraid of success. What if people disagree with what we're doing? What if you make the wrong decision? These questions are never-ending when we're focused on fear. Each of them has one thing in common—they keep us from achieving our goals.

Isn't it time you took control of your life? Isn't it time you rewrote the script, recognizing that it is possible to face your fears no matter what changes you need to go through?

Making a Change

You may be saying that you're fixed in your ways, you're too young, too old, too busy, too afraid to take the risk, and so on. Instead of embracing change and looking for ways to improve your life, you are adamant about staying where you are. You stick to your comfort zone. Never moving forward with your life, never progressing, never experiencing growth. There's a distinct difference between growth and change. You make changes by altering something about yourself or your situation. Think about relocating to another country or city, a change of address. Maybe you're trying to be more professional by having a complete makeover, a change. It's something that shifts from where you are now to somewhere completely different.

Change can occur gradually over time, or it can be something that happens relatively quickly. Getting married, divorced, or having a baby occurs on a specific day. Due to this kind of change, your life will never be the same again. You would have to plan for each of the events mentioned. They don't occur in a vacuum, but the actual event itself is something that's a once-off at the time. We don't always get the chance to prepare for imminent change. When a loved one dies unexpectedly, our lives will never be the same again. There's no way that you could ever prepare yourself for this kind of event.

Growth, on the other hand, has a much longer time frame. It's progressive. Think about starting a fitness regime because you want to improve your health. You won't simply become fit after your first 30-minute visit to the gym. It's going to take time to get there. You may need to change your diet and stop smoking (something that also does not happen overnight.)

You can't experience growth without changing your life, thoughts, behavior, or the direction your life is headed. Becoming more positive in life will mean changing negative thinking, negative self-talk, and even your mindset. To enjoy a positive lifestyle, you're going to constantly be aware of these changes every day.

It would be best if you had a reason for wanting to grow. Without this reason, you'll soon lose focus before experiencing all the benefits of growth. Growth is unsuccessful a lot of the time because making long-term changes can be tedious. We don't always see the results we're looking for, especially when it comes to growth. If we're not patient with ourselves and motivated to keep going, the growth we want will always remain just out of reach.

It's natural to be afraid of making long-term changes. Especially when there's no guarantee, you'll ever get to where you want to be. Although throwing in the towel shouldn't be an option. Working toward growth doesn't always have a deadline because it's progressive. Each change you make on your journey to ultimate growth needs action before it leads to any measure of success.

Action means being willing to do whatever it takes. It's the physical doing instead of adopting a wishing approach to reach your goals. You must be prepared to put in the work. This may mean spending more time in the office because you want to be promoted to a better position. Maybe it means attending evening classes or training courses to hone your skills in a particular direction. Suppose you plan on getting back to that fitness goal, and you're not prepared to put the time, effort, and energy into specific training or a regular fitness program you'll never get there. It might take you a year before you're satisfied with your progress. The moment you begin to see results, chances are you'll be motivated to keep pushing toward your ultimate goal.

How will you know whether you need to change or concentrate on growth instead? It will always be dependent on the ultimate goal you have in your sights. We've covered various examples above of the difference between the two. Manifesting abundance in your life and becoming the best version of yourself will take several long-term changes.

Take Action

Action implies that there's going to be work involved. Putting in work scares many of us because anything involving work usually means time and effort are needed. Because we live in an instant world, we feel entitled to our goals being reached miraculously quickly. Get real. There's no way we're going to get to where we want to be without both work and effort.

Instead of bitching and moaning about what you need to do, do it. Commit to yourself that you're prepared to do whatever is necessary to achieve your ultimate goals. I'm not saying that making these changes in your life will be a walk in the park. On the contrary, chances are they're going to be painful. They're going to test your willpower. There will be many days when you'd quite happily throw in the towel, and that's okay. Keep your eye on the prize.

Moving forward, one small step at a time is still progress. It's dragging your ass out of bed in the cold on a winter morning to hit the gym. You don't want to, but you know that achieving your goal weight means you need to. Maybe it's sacrificing carbohydrates, so you enjoy a healthier lifestyle or studying for hours to qualify for that promotion. It may mean attending months of couples therapy in an attempt to save your marriage. The big question is, what are you prepared to do today that will bring you closer to achieving your ultimate goal? Nobody said it would be easy. Nobody said it would be pain-free. Nobody said it would happen overnight. Unless you're prepared to put in the effort, you'll never be able to enjoy the benefits of growth. It's part of your personal development.

Like pieces on a chessboard, you'll never win unless you move the pieces forward deliberately. Sure, you're taking a calculated risk in how your opponent is going to react. But you can't just sit there waiting either. Life's exactly the same. Unless you're prepared to make a move, you'll continue to remain where you are. You're prepared to allow those around you to move ahead, which is almost always to our detriment.

Think about that promotion at the office. You've been after it for a while now, but so have a couple of your colleagues. Who do you think is going to secure the position? Someone who's actively doing something about being appointed to the post, or the person is sitting back waiting for it to happen. I know which I would prefer if I were the employer.

The truth is you've already experienced tremendous growth in your life. Cast your mind back to how much you grew between starting school and when you graduated. When you first started in the job market, you were green. Chances are you didn't know too much. You had to learn. Unfortunately, if you want to get anywhere in life, this learning and growth never end. I'm not saying there won't be a whole lot of obstacles in your path. You need to morph from where you are currently to where you eventually want to be. We don't learn and grow unless we're prepared to do something about it unless we're prepared to move in the direction of our dreams. We need our goals to be clearly defined. Without this, we'll remain stagnant.

Why would you want to remain in the same place? What's holding you back? If it happens to be fear, then it's time you get out of that rut. Fear can only do so much if we let it. Rather than allowing fear to keep you stagnant, it may be time to face up to it and decide to do what you want to do anyway. Because growth is incremental, you need to accept that it's not going to be instantaneous. Reaching your goals won't happen immediately. Unless you do something about them, it's unlikely you'll get to where you want to be at all.

When working toward a long-term goal it's easy to become complacent. It's easy to become frustrated because you're not seeing the results of each of the baby steps you're taking immediately. It's easy to cheat on that diet. After all, what's one little chocolate going to do? It's easy not to recognize that slow and steady progress is what's ultimately going to get you there.

As long as you're doing something every day that's going to inch you closer toward your goals then you're doing something worthwhile. You can compare reaching your goals to driving a car. Unless you put the key in the ignition and move through each of the gears, you can't expect to reach your destination. You have a starting point. You need to take action to progress.

You will need to gear up to get to where you want to be by accelerating. There may be times when you need to put your foot on the brakes for a moment or two. It's humanly impossible to keep your foot on the gas constantly. Just as run the risk of blowing your engine, you could physically hit burnout.

When you're tired or physically ill, you can't continue at the same pace; this is when you need to rest up and rejuvenate to reach your goals. Setting yourself big-ass goals that you know are humanly impossible will frustrate you and make you feel like a failure. They'll overwhelm you, making you feel like you're no longer in control. Feeling overwhelmed is one of those key reasons for giving up on your quest to achieve your goals.

Create a Routine Around Reaching Your Goals

Look for simple ways to get a routine together where you can spend a specific amount of time each day working specifically toward reaching your goals. Getting out of bed to work out each morning is part of a routine.

Spending 30-minutes to study each day is more productive than trying to cram in a couple of hours just before an important exam. You may be saying that indeed a couple of hours would be equivalent to more time. It doesn't mean that you will retain the same amount of information as you would be working at a steady, relaxed pace.

Do you have enough faith and conviction that you'll achieve the goals you've identified as being worthwhile? If you don't have this, then you're wasting your time. Your goals need to challenge you. They need to push you out of that comfort zone that many of us are terrified to step beyond. It's fear of the unknown. It's also completely understandable. I mean, none of us have a crystal ball that can predict the future.

There's no guarantee that we'll achieve the goals we've identified. However, you can count on the one thing by doing nothing; you're sure to stagnate. You'll remain exactly where you are. In the months and years to follow, you're sure to look back at your life and question why you're still in the same place when others around you are succeeding. The truth is that you decide whether you want to progress or be happy to accept whatever life is going to give you

The truth is that staying where you are is a cop-out. It's simply looking for an excuse to justify your inability to celebrate even the smallest of wins. So why then are you choosing to do this? Are you prepared to remain in the past when everyone around you is living in the present but focusing on the future? What's the payoff for staying where you are? I ask this question because for us to do anything in this life, there needs to be some motivating factor. Doing nothing with your life is still a choice. Taking no action is still a choice. Looking for excuses is still a choice.

Maybe you're too afraid of making a mistake, so you choose to stick to the safe side by doing nothing at all. The only way to move beyond this fear is by pushing through it. It may mean reassessing what you're doing. What's your plan? Do you know what the result is going to look like? Do you have a daily routine in place? If you do, it may be time for you to revisit your routine to make you stick with the plan.

Have you set aside specific times for these routines? Maybe it's first thing in the morning for 30-minutes and another 30-minutes before retiring. Instead of being vague about these times, be clear about exact times. If you plan to get up at 5 am to be at the gym by 5.30 am for an hour's workout, you need to stick with it. If you've decided to plan for the following day each night before retiring, then be specific. Set aside time between 9 pm and 9.30 pm to get this done.

Don't deviate from your plan unless something critical comes up. And yes, life happens. Do yourself a favor and be on the lookout for things you may be doing each day to procrastinate. All that procrastination will achieve is to rob you of precious time where you could have been doing something constructive. You could have been working on something that's going to bring you closer to your goals.

Procrastination breaks your stride. You'll know that you're procrastinating if you're wasting countless hours on social media. Maybe you spend a fair amount of time shuffling paperwork instead of touching it once. This way, you get to deal with it and get it out the way. Notice that the words used here are all negative. You are wasting time, spending time. You should be looking at investing your time wisely instead.

Isn't it time to put things into perspective when it comes to working at your goals? Look at the bigger picture instead of being myopic. It's not just about the here and now. Sure, this time is important because what you do now will affect you in the future. The most significant difference is that if you don't know where you want to be if you don't have clearly defined goals, there's no chance of you ever getting there. Shift your focus to the future

Chapter 7:

Living the Law

What is the Law of Attraction

The Law of Attraction can help you get everything you want from life. You are the one that should be in control of what you get out of life. That's what each of the chapters leading to this point has been about. We're going to talk about developing healthy habits further on. Suffice it to say that when you're living your life according to the law of attraction, you've implemented practices that will help you achieve the health, wealth, happiness, and success you truly desire.

Most successful people have figured out that there are steps necessary for their continued success. There's no end to what you can do when you put your mind to it. You can harness the power of the universe to help you achieve whatever your heart desires. You can strengthen relationships, manifest love, joy, peace, or whatever else you concentrate on.

A word of caution. If you're constantly negative, or your thoughts keep on going there then don't be too surprised if that's what you continue experiencing. The truth is that whatever you spend your time thinking about will manifest in the present. When you focus on a shortage of things or lack, that's exactly what you'll receive more of. This is one of the reasons why you need to break free from that mold.

Your focus needs to shift from only seeing the bad to concentrating on all the good things life has to offer. If you're currently battling with something, maybe it's time to question where your thoughts are—struggling with excess weight? Perhaps it's time to stop fixating on weight and think about all the things you'll enjoy when you're slim. Think about what you will look like wearing that outfit you've had your eye on. What are you doing to help you focus on achieving this goal?

It all boils down to what you believe about yourself and the world around you. It's said that what you think about most of the time is what you'll attract to your life. When you constantly feel that you're in trouble financially, your financial woes will continue, even if you keep thinking that you don't want debt. You're still transferring your thoughts onto debt. You should rather be thinking about prosperity and wealth. Because of the power of positive thinking, there should be no place in your vocabulary for negativity, especially when it comes to negative thoughts. Anything that crosses your mind that you pay too much attention to will end up happening. Have you ever had a concern about your health, to the point where you become paranoid? Chances are, you'll soon develop symptoms that are in line with the illness.

Do you permit yourself to dare to dream of a better future? Or do you believe deep down that you don't deserve success? To reach any goals that are worthwhile pursuing means taking the time to dream of a better future. It means visualizing what you want and believing that you can have what you wish to without any reservations.

The moment you begin to question anything, your dreams will be diminished, and no matter what you do, you'll never get what you want. Your dreams should motivate you to take whatever action is necessary. It's all about what you hold onto in your mind. Are you prepared to believe in a better future for yourself? Do you recognize that you can grow if you put your mind to it?

Where Does the Law of Attraction Come From?

The law of attraction is similar to the law of gravity. It exists on a metaphysical level. You can't see it, you can't touch it, but it's there. This law has always been around. Ancient philosophers realized there was a connection between our thoughts and how this influenced our behavior and, ultimately, our lives.

If this law is there and real, then it makes perfect sense for us to use it to our full advantage. When you stop and think about it, what do you have to lose? You have everything to gain if it works. Using this law to your advantage will help you reach any goal you desire as long as you use it correctly.

What can you manifest with this law? It's pretty simple. You can manifest anything in any area of your life. Many people mistakenly believe that it's all about money or relationships. While this may be true, there's so much more to the law of attraction. Anything you can imagine can manifest itself in your life when you set a clear intention that it's what you want. You may want that promotion at work, change your lifestyle to a healthier one. Maybe you want to strengthen your current relationship by practicing patience.

The point is that anything you can visualize and set your intention toward will be what will manifest. If you're focused on just one area of your life, you may end up feeling as though something is missing. When working with the Law of Attraction, it's best to balance your goals and intentions across each area of your life. Your mindset needs to be focused on growth rather than feeling that you're limited in what you can achieve. Remember that growth occurs over an extended period instead of just the here and now. A growth mindset is open to new ideas and experiences.

Are the doubts running through your head holding you back? Maybe you've never really noticed because you aren't paying close attention to your thinking. If this is the case, then you need to rectify this. With an average of 40,000 thoughts going through our minds daily, it's easy to get lost. It becomes increasingly difficult to sift through the positive and the negative. If you want the Law of Attraction to affect your life positively, you need to distinguish between this thinking. Negative thinking directed inward toward us feeds our limiting beliefs. These are all the negative beliefs we have about ourselves, usually originating from past experiences. Negative thinking produces negative energy, which continues to attract negativity into your life.

Vibrational Energy and Frequencies

Energies vibrate at different frequencies. The more positive the emotions, the higher the vibrational frequency, whereas negative emotions vibrate at lower energy levels. The thing about these frequencies and energy levels is that they rub off on others. That's why when you're in the company of negative individuals for an extended period, you end up joining in their pity party. You can't help it because they're transmitting those bad vibes.

Negative energies are present whenever we're angry, frustrated, confused, bored, hurt, anxious, depressed, worried, guilty, overwhelmed—you get the picture. You'll agree that none of these feelings are great. They make us feel worse about life and the situations we find ourselves in. Then again, feelings of optimism, passion, excitement, peace, love, happiness, joy, gratitude, abundance, hope, compassion, prosperity, and any other good vibe are what you should be after.

We can only achieve a positive outcome in our lives when we choose these frequencies instead of those that seem to drain us. Have you ever noticed how negative people drain the very life force out of you while happy people exude confidence and optimism wherever they go? For some reason, you love being around them because they make you feel good about yourself; this is where attraction comes into play. We're attracted to the same kind of energy we're sending out into the universe. It's quite simple. If you're having a hard time and you can't seem to get out of a funk, maybe it's time to take a look at who you're associating with. It may not be possible to suddenly sever all ties with every single negative person in your life. Maybe they're a close family, and it's just not possible.

Something to remember about negative people is that you'll have to work that much harder to shift their vibrational energy even slightly. On the other hand, it doesn't take much for us to be dragged down with them. For some reason, negative vibes are that much more powerful. It makes sense then that you try to keep yourself isolated from these people as much as possible. You want to be successful, happy, healthy, and wealthy. You want to build those lasting relationships. The only way you can do this is by setting a positive intention that you want out of life.

There's no room for negativity because that will derail all your plans. There's no room for even a single doubt in your abilities when it comes to getting what you want. The moment you question whether or not you can do something, whether or not you deserve something, you've lost. Remember that whatever you're thinking, good or bad, is what you'll experience.

You're probably asking how the hell you can tell whether you're positive or negative? How do you know what energy you're giving off? That's the problem. That's why so many people end up in a rut. The truth is that all that's happening is in response to whatever vibrations are around you. You're simply reacting to the vibrational energy of others instead of being more aware of your thoughts and emotions. If you can't get a grip on these, there's no way to be in control of where your life is headed. You're happy to go with the flow. You're satisfied with your life as it is. How do you ever expect to get anywhere with your life when you're not even aware of your thoughts and emotions?

Being stuck in the quagmire of mediocrity is simple. You don't even need to do anything to get there. Mediocrity is taking the easy way out. At least you'll have a lot of company because it's one of the main reasons why so many people give up on their hopes and dreams. They haven't made a clear decision about what they want. Lack of clarity is the same as confusion, which is on the lower end of the vibrational scale. This negative energy loops on what seems to be a never-ending cycle. The result is always the same because there doesn't seem to be a way out.

It's like a plane sitting in a holding pattern, waiting to land. Unless the control tower gives the signal, it will stay right there (as long as it has the necessary fuel, of course.) So many choose to live their lives this way, being complacent with where they are. Life is boring. You can't feel fulfilled because you're not getting anywhere. It's being stuck in the same mundane, brain-numbing job for years on end. You're not happy, but you're also not prepared to do anything about it. It's too hard. You believe you're too old, too young, not clever enough, too clever, and so it goes. It's your reality, and until you do something about it, nothing is ever going to change.

You're stuck in a toxic relationship, but you're too afraid to do anything about it. What if you never find anyone else who will love you? Better the devil you know than the one you don't. Relationships are hard work. Starting over is unpredictable. Sure, you can hang onto each of these excuses to stay where you are, but you're miserable in doing so.

Everything in life is risky. There comes a time when you need to throw caution to the wind because where you are is killing you. You're probably desperately unhappy, and once again, these emotions are all negative. You're attracting a life devoid of any happiness or joy. You're more comfortable living in denial rather than even trying to redesign your life to the way you want it to be.

Visualize and State Your Intentions

Suppose you want to live a different life from the one you have now. You need to change your mindset. The way you think, and what you believe in. Do you want to know what the key to abundance and the Law of Attraction is? It is believing that you can have whatever you want from life. You can have the relationship you want, the career you want. In short, there's nothing you can't achieve if you set your mind to it.

You have to believe you deserve all the great things that the universe can offer you. Believe that you're worthy of receiving positive things into your life. As you shift your focus toward each of these things, you'll notice how things begin to change. Because you've changed the vibrational energy you're giving off; these positive changes will manifest in your life.

If you want to keep experiencing positive things in your life, then it's time to change your thought patterns. Where are you focusing your energy? That's what the universe is responding to. The universe will reward you with whatever you're constantly thinking about. Being aware of every thought, emotion, and vibration you're sending into the universe is the only way to change your current reality. Getting there means removing all forms of negative thinking from your life. I'm not saying that this is going to be easy or that it will happen overnight. It's going to take a lot of effort to keep your thinking under control. You're going to need to change your self-talk. You know, the voices in your head that kind of take over when you least expect them to.

These voices in your head are responsible for everything that happens to you. Good and bad. Your thoughts are responsible for those movies that play over and over in your head, the never-ending loop. Be careful not to think about the negatives; this won't result in a positive outcome. Guaranteed, you'll just get more of exactly what you don't want. The universe can't tell the difference. It simply responds to what you're thinking about. Put it this way, if you send out the vibration that you want to get out of debt, all the universe responds to is debt. Your entire thinking needs to shift to the positive. Focus on prosperity or wealth instead. Think about what financial freedom will feel like. Pretty good, right? Think about everything you'll enjoy with your wealth. Keep your thoughts there. Don't be surprised if things fall apart when you start thinking about having no debt again. It's all about the stories we tell ourselves.

Have you got a clear picture in your mind of precisely what you want? How clear are these images? For the law of attraction to become a reality in your life, you should visualize what you desire. The only word of advice here is that you need to be realistic about your expectations. Yes, the universe will respond to whatever you focus on consistently but expecting to own a Porsche in the next three months when you're currently unemployed isn't realistic at all. Set positive intentions around each of the goals you've identified as being practical and worthwhile. Get rid of the self-talk that's holding you back.

Are your thoughts, intentions, and self-talk aligned? It would help if you mastered this important aspect of the Law of Attraction. You need to project your goals for the future so that you imagine yourself already in possession of whatever it is you desire. You want that perfect relationship. How is it going to make you feel once you have it? That dream home? What will it be like living there? Can you feel the power of the engine in that new car you want to own? Having anything you want is on the other side of your thinking.

Maybe you battle to stay positive. Your thoughts keep defaulting back to those pesky negative ones. Remember I said that negative thinking is so much easier than actively focusing on remaining positive. Positivity takes constant effort. You can move this along with the help of positive affirmations. Changing how you feel is central to the law of attraction working for you rather than against you. Feeling good about yourself and the life you want will help get you there.

Don't overthink it. If you know what you want and how it will make you feel, it's time to communicate with the universe. State your affirmation to the universe and leave it there. A lot of us fail at stating our affirmations. We keep on wanting to go back and change things. Self-doubt creeps into our thinking, and this will work against us. It will be just the thing to keep us from having the life we want—the life we truly deserve.

Cultivate gratitude for all the things you currently have. This thinking will help to increase your vibrational energy. Being grateful is a powerful tool in the arsenal of life. It doesn't mean working hard at it either. Try and express gratitude for even the smallest of things. Doing this will make you more aware of your surroundings. You'll be able to recognize the good things flowing into your life. Find something to be grateful for every single day.It may seem like a straightforward solution, that's because it is. Getting into the habit of being grateful and looking for something different each day will lead to being mindful about what's happening around you. Changing your outlook toward life and shift your mood.

Take the time to greet a stranger, thank someone for excellent service, and help a neighbor. It's pausing to recognize all the good in your life, things like nature, close friends, loved ones, family. There's so much good to be had in the world, and because we get so wrapped up in our little world, we fail to recognize it. We are blind to the fact that there's way more good out there once you begin looking. All we need to do is take the time to find it. Once we do, we should celebrate the joy this brings into our lives.

The law of attraction has the power to change a life that's currently ordinary into something extraordinary. It can manifest everything you've ever wanted as long as you believe it's possible. That belief needs to be unwavering. Don't doubt for a minute that you deserve whatever you desire. Replace any doubts you may have with faith in the process. Believe in yourself.

Chapter 8:

Loving Yourself

Let's face it, loving yourself and putting yourself first is hard to do. We're much harder on ourselves than anyone else. We're prepared to overlook mistakes made by others yet expect perfection in everything we do. For some reason, we hold ourselves to a much higher standard.

We'll do things for others, no matter whether they're family or strangers. We are often going out of our way to do so. It usually comes at the expense of our own time; that's such a precious commodity. We inconvenience ourselves, say yes when we really ought to be saying no. Our own needs are placed somewhere at the bottom of our list of priorities.

We waste countless hours trying to change who we are to fit into the cookie-cutter mold of what society dictates. The importance we place on the relationships we have with others overshadows the relationship we have with ourselves. The relationship with ourselves is sometimes non-existent. Then we wonder why we're so unhappy, why we are anxious and depressed. We wonder why our lives feel so out of control.

The truth is that before you can have a lasting relationship with anyone else, you need first to learn to love yourself. It's choosing to do what's best for you, placing your own needs first for a change. Instead of investing so much time getting to know others, how about taking the time to get to know what's important to you.

Stop Comparing Yourself

Loving yourself all begins with accepting yourself just the way you are. Far too often, we want to be just like someone else. We want the things we believe they have. This is perception rather than reality. It's what we see on the surface. We look at their picture-perfect lives, all the while judging ourselves, blaming ourselves, criticizing ourselves for not having all the STUFF they have.

They're better looking than we are, more educated, more successful, more accomplished, more, well, more everything. Instead of being real about all the things we've done in our lives, we choose to criticize ourselves. We look past our success, everything we have, and everything that makes us who we are.

Getting to the place where we can look at ourselves in the mirror, see who we are, and accept ourselves is tough. Acceptance means being able to acknowledge that it's okay to have faults and flaws. It means coming to terms with our reality and not shaping your life around one imposed by others.

We need to accept that there's nothing wrong with wanting to do something more with your life. There's nothing wrong with wanting to progress and grow. As long as we do it for ourselves, on our terms, and not please anyone else. People-pleasing is one of the barriers that stand between you being who you're meant to be.

It's looking for a mask to hide behind. And yes, we all have masks that we interchange to meet the needs of a situation. The problem with wearing a mask is we lose our authentic selves in the process. We're so busy trying to live someone else's life.

Do you even know who you are under all the layers of bullshit you keep on telling yourself? The problem with all these lies is that we believe them. We allow them to shape us and determine our future. We become overly concerned with how others see us rather than how we see ourselves. We are so worried about making mistakes that may influence what people think about us that we either don't do anything or behave completely out of character.

When it comes to making mistakes, it's good to remember that we're all human at the end of the day. We're all unique. Stop comparing yourself to others. Don't for one second think that anyone out there achieves success in their lives without making mistakes. It's the way we learn. Without trial and error, no one could ever achieve any degree of success. However, you can't let the fear and paranoia of doing something wrong prevent you from living the life you deserve either.

The moment you question whether you're deserving of all the universe has to offer, that's what will continue to manifest itself. Doubt, insecurity, and fear are all feelings. Negative feelings will translate into low vibrational energy. All that's going to manifest is more of the same. Can you see the detrimental effect these emotions can have on your life?

Let Go of Fear

Isn't it time you faced up to the fears you have about being enough? Good enough, clever enough, successful enough. The truth is that no matter how good you are or what sort of success you achieve in your life, there will always be someone better than you. Someone more intelligent than you, richer than you. Someone who has a better-looking spouse, and so on. That's just a fact of life.

Don't let these fears take hold of you. According to the law of attraction, fear is possibly one of the worst feelings you can hold onto. It's sure to keep you from not only living the life you deserve but having all those things you want to have. It will keep you from achieving your goals. It will only result in a life where you're constantly on edge, one where you're out of control, never quite certain of yourself.

Fear is the opposite of belief. Without believing you're confident and adopting a confident attitude, it's unlikely you'll move past these feelings, feelings that are keeping you away from an abundant life—question each of your fears to discover whether they're valid. Try and identify where they come from. Is there something from your past that's causing you to feel this way? When that happens, and you find the trigger for believing what you believe, it's necessary to deal with it most efficiently.

Don't get me wrong. There's no such thing as a quick fix to these negative beliefs. I wish there were because it would be easier to move beyond the barriers we create ourselves. When you discover sufficient confidence deep within yourself, it becomes easier to display the willpower necessary to move beyond the fear. The willpower needed to put your goals and your needs first. And no, this isn't a selfish attitude to adopt. If you're not prepared to worry about yourself, you really cannot expect anyone else to be all that concerned about you either.

Be Kind to Yourself

Another key recommendation is to be kind to yourself. Realize that you're not going to get there on your own, and as much as you hate asking for help, maybe it's time. Chances are you have been raised with the belief that you either need to "man up," or that "big girls don't cry." The truth is that this isn't always possible. Life gets to all of us at some stage or another. We aren't really wired to continue like a robot constantly. There has to be some downtime—time for you to recharge and rejuvenate. Even the most put-together person you know takes time out on the off occasion for them to come to terms with exactly where their life is now and where they're heading.

There are slight course corrections if adjustments need to be made to the course they're on. All factors are considered, especially the current path you're on and where it's likely to lead. If you know you need to make changes because you've done something wrong, find the best possible solution and move forward. Try not to break your momentum. Most of all, be kind and patient with who you are. Nobody expects you to make changes after night. Instead, significant changes take a lot longer than just a few moments. Be realistic in what you expect yourself to do. Without this, you're only setting yourself up to fail and fail horribly.

There's a crazy effect that those around you bring into your life. It's not always good either. The truth is that we sometimes care more about the way others view us. We care about how they perceive the things we do. We worry about whether or not we'll receive their stamp of approval in everything we do. Why the hell would you want to do this? What's so important about getting the approval of those around you? What's so important about how they think of you?

We all want to be liked and trusted. We all want to be accepted by society. Those closest to us, friends, our family, our work colleagues, our managers, and so the list goes on. Quite frankly, even the way total strangers view us influences our behavior. We fret incessantly over their opinions of us. What are they thinking? Do we have their approval and support on the things we're currently doing? Are there things we need to change to earn this approval?

Of course, when trying to get the approval of others, not everyone will be onboard. There will always be those who would like for nothing more than to see us fall on our asses. They don't want us to succeed because it may mean doing better than them. It may mean they can no longer hold their success over you. They may want to be keeping you in that holding pattern because it suits their own selfish needs. These individuals are toxic, and as with anything toxic, you need to avoid it like the plague (excuse the pun). If you can identify toxic tendencies with those you're associating with, the only antidote to this is by cutting them loose. Minimize your contact with these people so they don't succeed in dragging you down with them.

We've already spoken about the fact that it's so much easier coming to terms with negativity and doom and gloom rather than being upbeat. We're often afraid to let these toxic people go. We don't want to be labeled as a snob or thinking we're better than them. The truth is that spending time with these individuals will drain you of all the energy you have at your disposal. These people not only thrive on being miserable themselves. They aren't that happy unless they've made everyone else around them miserable as well

Take Charge

Don't be afraid to take charge of your life. Let others know what you're made of, especially when it comes to working toward your hopes and dreams. Live your life in such a way that people are acutely aware that you're going after exactly what you want. It's one of the few ways that you'll earn the respect of others and be given the support and possibly additional tools you need to get to where you want to be.

If you're not in charge of your own life, charting your course toward the destiny of your choosing, how do you expect to get there? Nobody is going to do it for you, and riding on the coattails of others is only going to get you to actively work toward someone else's dreams rather than your own. No matter how great someone else's goals or dreams maybe, you'll never feel as though you've accomplished anything when the goals you're working toward belong to someone else.

Discover the secret to putting yourself in the driver's seat. How can you put yourself first so that you're in control of what's happening in your life? Putting yourself first means assuming control, you know, that thing we spoke about earlier. You have to be responsible for where your life is headed. If you're not happy with it, then it's pretty much up to you to change it. Don't wait until the changes become critical. Where you're virtually paralyzed because you know you've made a ton of mistakes in getting to where you want to be. Remember that change and failure result in some of life's greatest lessons. Without these two realities, we'd have nothing to aim for. Everyone in life will just be cruising through without any motivation to do better, be better, or do something more with your life.

Of course, failure is going to bring with it a certain degree of pain. As with most lessons in life, change means there's pain attached. We've already mentioned that nobody's perfect. So why expect perfection from yourself. There's simply no way you're going to be able to achieve anything in life without falling down a couple of times. The secret to failure is having the willpower and ability to get up. It's choosing not to allow these failures to prevent you from trying to make a difference not only in your own life but possibly in the world.

Tap into previous experiences so you can draw from these mistakes. You don't want to keep repeating those things you've done in the past that have held you back. That's just a pointless exercise. When we were much younger, the fear of failure wasn't present. It becomes more prevalent the older we get. Failure is uncomfortable. It's messy, and it means hard work to move forward. That's okay, though, because at least you have the chance of moving forward.

One of the only ways for us to progress is to rewrite our story. We have the power to make whatever we want out of our lives as long as we're prepared to learn important life lessons. Without doing this, chances are we'll remain precisely where we are. That's not what life is about. It's not what we're meant to be doing with each of the opportunities presented to us.

Life will always offer us various opportunities, just like the vast selection of goodies we have in a convenience store. We're allowed to pick and choose which of these opportunities resonate within us. Which of these opportunities are we prepared to select as something to focus our effort on? How much effort is enough? And, which of the myriad of opportunities will be the right ones to be concentrating on?

So, what happens if you don't see these opportunities around you? Nothing seems to be gelling. No opportunities seem to be beating down your door. Maybe it's time to look for things you can do that will draw you closer to achieving the goals you want. If we're waiting for the perfect timing before we attempt anything, then chances are we'll be waiting for an extended period. There's no time like the present. Think about it for a moment. Not every opportunity is always apparent. Many times, they come wrapped in defeat, in rejection, in failure. Of course, failure consists of a fair amount of pain.

Life Yourself Up

I cannot stress how important it is to learn the lessons behind the pain of failure. Get your emotions and your feelings under control. Don't be afraid to feel pain but beware of holding onto it so thoroughly that you cannot experience happiness and joy. These are opposite to the negativity of pain. They also operate on two completely different frequencies and energy levels. Pain and fear are some of the lowest frequencies, while you can find joy and happiness at a much higher frequency. Question your motives. By identifying how you feel, you'll have a much better understanding of exactly where your energy levels are. If you happen to be feeling low rather than full of energy, then chances are there's something negative that's blocking your energy or holding you back. Typical of this kind of scenario is suffering from anxiety because you feel overwhelmed by situations surrounding your life. Nobody promised that things will always go exactly the way we want them to go.

When facing these challenges, you have a couple of choices available to you. Either you can give in, allowing yourself to become consumed with worry, guilt, stress, insecurity, and all sorts of other negative emotions, or you can choose to do something about it. It would be best if you found some means of releasing this tension. Releasing tension isn't always easy to do. Sometimes it means doing a complete 180 degrees with your life. It may mean becoming bold and daring and getting out there to meet new people, taking up a sport or hobby that you never really thought of before. You need to grab life with both hands, without fear. Choose to make something more of your life than being held back by things you don't necessarily have control over.

Learning to love yourself means taking the time you need to begin to feel good about yourself. It's putting yourself first without all the guilt. So many times, we focus on self-sacrifice. For some reason, we think that self-sacrifice on behalf of others is a noble thing to do. The truth is that the longer you're paying attention to making someone else's life better, the less time you're working toward your own life. If you don't take care of yourself, nobody else is going to.

If you're feeling overwhelmed by all the things you need to do, things you need to change, sacrifices you need to make, then it may mean forcing yourself to take some time out (without feeling guilty about it.) This guilt is what prevents us from doing this. We're so convinced that we're invincible, that we just need to push through and keep going that we often fail to see all the warning signs out there that we're heading toward severe burnout.

Instead of forcing yourself just to keep going, take the time you need to recharge. Maybe this means unplugging for a while. Force yourself to take some downtime. Perhaps this means binging on watching movies all day as a means of escape. Maybe it means spending the day in your PJs, sleeping, or leaving all the household chores that you'd generally be beating yourself up about. Don't even feel guilty about this. All that guilt will do is escalate an already frustrating situation.

All of these things culminate in you taking the time to care for yourself. Consider that without doing this, you could be headed toward more serious consequences. Ones where your long-term health can suffer because you were too stubborn to take the odd break once in a while. We'll cover a series of habits and routines that can help you recharge daily in the final chapter.

Put Yourself First

You may be thinking that these decisions and choices are flawed because you're focusing on yourself. You may have been taught that this isn't healthy. It's selfish and means that you're not prepared to dedicate that time to others. Stop thinking like this. The truth is that you'll be of no use to anyone when you're spiraling downward. Loving yourself sets you up for success in your life. You can once again be totally in control of who you are and what you're doing. It's living your life on your terms instead of doing it to please other people. You get the chance to live a life that's accomplished, rather than one where you doubt everything you do.

It's putting yourself first ahead of everyone else. In most instances, we place ourselves right at the bottom of our list of priorities. We'll do everything to please our family, friends, colleagues, managers, and often even strangers. While this is noble and a great attitude to have, it serves no purpose when we're at the bottom of the list. You can't possibly expect to have the energy necessary to please all of these other people when you can't even care for yourself. Treating yourself like this only shows how little regard you have for yourself. It's an indication of low self-esteem and a lack of self-confidence. If you're currently guilty of feeling this way or behaving this way, you need to look at how you view yourself carefully.

You need to love yourself first before trying to love those around you. This chapter has been all about the consequences of placing others before yourself. You are doing everything to please them at your own expense. That's precisely the reality of the situation. By placing them first, or even ahead of yourself, you can't expect your own life to go exactly the way you want it to go. Perhaps you feel there's a gaping hole somewhere. Maybe you think you need to go out of your way to earn the love and affection of others. When you love yourself and put yourself first, you no longer need this validation from others. You can move through your life confidently, without needing to please others or waiting for them to permit you to do the things you want to do.

Loving yourself means accepting who you are just as you are now. You don't need to jump through a whole lot of hoops to prove yourself worthy of being accepted by others. It's genuinely believing that you deserve everything you're working toward without exception. You love yourself unconditionally, rather than wanting to be just like someone else.

It's living your own life on your terms. The way I view self-love and self-care might be entirely different from the way you view it, and that's okay. You need to do what's best for you, rather than what's expected by society. Take time out from judging yourself too harshly. Judging yourself is usually where the comparison to everyone else comes in. it's not only unhealthy, but it will prevent you from achieving your goals time and time again.

Life constantly seems to be a never-ending competition. We compete in the workplace. We compete for our attention, whether it's from our loved ones or even those we know. We want to be the best, but often this is for completely the wrong reasons. We are usually doing it as a means of wanting to do better than the next person. This belief is flawed. The only person we should be competing with is ourselves. After all, we're the ones we have to live with.

We're responsible for all the self-talk happening in our heads. The moment these focus on the negative continuously, the more trouble we're in. It's these limiting beliefs that keep us stuck in the present and hold us back from everything life has to offer. You don't need the approval of others before you can have anything and everything you desire.

Chapter 9:

Healthy Habits

One thing about habits is that we all have them. Whether they're good or bad, they tend to follow us around wherever we go. They can help us accomplish great things, or they can hold us back because they're unhealthy. The good news is that regardless of where we are now, we each have the power to make changes to bad habits and replace them with those habits that will get us to where we want to be.

How Habits are Developed Over Time

When Thinking about the habits we already have, you don't even need to think about doing them; you just do. Your entire morning routine is something that's done on autopilot. I mean, how often do you have to think about getting out of bed, putting one foot into a shoe after another, how to take a shower, or making yourself that early morning coffee. In all honesty, you don't.

Once you place the key in the ignition on your car, you automatically buckle up (or you should do.) You don't need to think about checking whether it's safe enough for you to pull into the road. You automatically do it because it's going to keep you safe. When you're thirsty, you don't plan on making that cup of tea. It happens without giving it a second thought. There are thousands of examples of things you've learned to do throughout your life that you now do without even thinking. Sure, when you first started, you were more cautious about being more intentional with your actions. Think about the first time you got behind the wheel of a car. Things were strange and unfamiliar to you. But the more you practiced, the more you performed each of the actions needed to drive a vehicle, the more natural it became.

When you're aware of your current habits, you can approach changing any habits that are detrimental to your life right now or implementing new habits that will improve your overall well-being and current lifestyle. There are many things we've got into the habit of doing that influence the outcome of our lives.

Not all of these are on the list of obvious things that are bad for us, things like smoking or drinking way more than we should. The truth is that any form of addictive behavior stands between us and habits that will lead to a healthy lifestyle. When it comes to these, the secret lies in moderation. Moderation means considering anything from the amount of food we eat or the types of food we choose to put in our mouths. Maybe it's being addicted to TV, the internet, and even social media. You may not believe that social media can hurt our lives, but it does. If you're in the habit of stopping everything you're doing to check your phone each time you receive a notification, you have a problem. Hey, some people get up in the middle of the night to check their phones. If this describes you, then maybe it's time to do something about breaking this destructive habit. Don't be afraid of switching your notifications off.

Set aside a specific amount of time each day to permit yourself to go through your social media accounts. Once you've set these limits, do everything in your power to stick with them. Don't be tempted to move the barriers out, don't push the time limits because you get caught up in the moment. It can happen so quickly. If you battle with this, initially, maybe you need to move your phone out of reach, lock it away until you get to the point when you're used to not even looking at it. Give yourself a break by getting off of social media altogether for a while. You'd be amazed by how much more positive you feel. One of the reasons for this is that you will no longer feel like you have to compete with everyone around you.

Changing Your Habits to Build a Healthy Lifestyle

You need to be realistic with attempting to change any of your existing habits. There's a straightforward way of trying to introduce new, healthier habits to your day. That's by attaching a new habit to something you're already doing. There are a couple of examples of doing this. Try and look for things you're already doing that are effectively dead time. An example of this would be when you're brushing your teeth. It's pretty easy for you to stick a couple of positive affirmations to the bathroom mirror. While you're brushing your teeth, you could be reading these to make them part of your day.

Other habits that involve dead time are when you're driving. The chances are that you feel frustrated that instead of using this time for more constructive and positive things, you're stuck in the car. One of these things could include finding something that's positive and uplifting. There are tons of great audiobooks available. Add these to your collection and listen to them. The result will be that your blood pressure will remain constant instead of feeling like you're about to burst a blood vessel whenever someone happens to cut in front of you or applies their brakes suddenly. You'll simply be taking things in your stride. It will do wonders for your overall mood and set the tone for the rest of your day.

The secret to changing your habits or adding new ones to those you already have is making sure they are broken down as far as possible. Be realistic about what you're able to handle. The moment things feel forced, or there are too many components, you're likely to fail, which leads to frustration, and in all likelihood, you'll throw the towel in. You want to avoid this point. You want to be sufficiently motivated to keep going. The only way to do this is for each of these habits to be so teeny tiny that you can't fail. If you're currently reading the newspaper while having your first cup of coffee in the morning, or watching the news, consider finding some other reading material that will inspire you to make positive changes in your life.

How much time are you wasting trying to find something to wear at the beginning of each day? You can do a couple of things to eliminate all this busy time, or should I rather say time being wasted. The first is to find something to wear the night before when you're not stressed about how long you're taking or focused on getting out the door. Something else you can do is consider buying several of the same outfits. There are a couple of really successful entrepreneurs and world leaders who adopted this habit. If you don't believe me, go back into the archives and take a look at what Steve Jobs used to wear every single day. Yes, people got used to his iconic black turtleneck sweater and jeans. Mark Zuckerberg wears blue t-shirts and jeans. Even Barack Obama had a closet full of blue suits. Indeed if it's good enough for each of these people, it's worth giving it a try. I mean, what do you have to lose—other than the frustration of having to decide under pressure. Think of everything you'll be able to do with the time you save.

One of the best habits you can incorporate into your daily routine is spending some time planning for your day. It doesn't matter whether you do this the night before retiring or in the morning before you start your day. It not only sets the right tone for the day, but you'll be more organized with what you're doing. Instead of just making a list of things to do, why not prioritize those things that are important when drawing up this list. Although there's nothing wrong with doing this in the morning, it's way more effective at night, giving you enough time to process your tasks mentally long before the time.

Before you even attempt to establish new habits, think about what you're currently capable of. There's no point in trying to do way more than is humanly possible or possible for you to handle right now. Life is pretty stressful with all the demands constantly pulling at us from every angle. There's only one way to prevent placing additional stress on your shoulders by introducing new habits. How aware are you of your current limitations? If you aren't, then maybe it's time to start taking stock of the habits you have at the moment. To be sure that you're paying attention to habits alone, it may mean spending a fair amount of time monitoring everything you do. Things like, what time are you getting up in the morning? What is your immediate routine once you're awake? Do you go for a morning run, collect the newspaper, switch on the coffee machine, let your animals out, wake up the kids? Keep track of everything you do and how long it usually takes you.

Change Won't Come Easy

Look at incorporating only those new habits you know are currently possible without adding additional stress. The whole point of introducing healthy habits into your lifestyle is to reduce stress in your life, not creating more. We each face different types of anxiety and challenges. Some of these are financial. Some are related to relationship woes. We worry about our children. We may have health issues that prevent us from doing all the things we'd rather be doing. Maybe we're unemployed, or we've just started a new business. Each of these things has the potential to cause us tremendous stress.

Consider what sort of time constraints you have to include a variety of new things. Is it humanly possible for you to incorporate them into your current schedule without being too disruptive? The last thing you need is to add in too many things too soon. Be realistic with your expectations. There are only so many hours in a day, and expect to push the envelope when it comes to getting things done can do nothing more than add to existing stress levels; you want to avoid this. You want habits that are going to make your life easier, not more complicated.

When looking for new habits to link to existing habits, look for things that suit your current lifestyle. If you hate exercising, it doesn't make sense to try and incorporate a strict exercise regime. You're bound to give up before you even get started. It will discourage you and may even put you off incorporating new habits altogether. The whole point of each of these new habits is to add value to your current lifestyle, not detract from it.

If you're not sure what will fit into your existing routine, then it's time to assess what you're currently doing. Think about all the things you enjoy doing. It's when you know where you are now that you can begin to move toward including activities that complement existing morning or evening routines. Once you've set your mind to include new things in your routine, it's worth getting these potential new habits in writing. Consider including meditation, yoga, exercise, or journaling into your morning routine. Schedule specific times to get each of these things done.

Morning routines can prepare you for the day ahead. An excellent way to complement each of these is by incorporating music. Doing this can increase your energy levels, especially when your chosen music is a high energy, with an uplifting beat. Keep away from music that's likely to bring you down or make you feel depressed. Match your music to the activity you're busy with. If you happen to be doing Yoga first thing in the morning or at nighttime, you'll be wanting to find music that's calming. For high-intensity workouts, something with a lot of energy behind it or music with a beat is better suited. Even when you sleep at night, you may want to listen to the calming sounds of waves crashing over rocks or forest sounds. These are just some of the ways you can incorporate music into your day.

Don't reinvent the wheel when it comes to trying to develop new habits. Take a look at where you are right now and start where you are. Add each new habit to an existing one. Be consistent in what you're doing; this is one of the few ways you can ensure that your habits stick. To be prepared to take on new habits, you need to be as individual and unique as you are. Focus on your mental, physical, and emotional wellbeing. New habits don't have to be introduced all at once. That's likely to place you under a lot of pressure, which you're trying to avoid. You want any new habits to make your life happier and easier wherever you can.

We're all aware of most of the everyday habits that most people focus on whenever they think about stacking or adding healthy habits. Some of these include drinking enough water, eating healthier, getting enough exercise daily, sleeping enough at night, journaling, meditation, and so on. Sure, there are distinct benefits to adding these to your routine. Don't get me wrong. I'm not knocking any of these. The thing is, what if you're already doing each of these things? Does this mean you're done, and there's nothing more you can add to enhance your life? Absolutely not.

Look at what's happening in your life right now. Are you still feeling stressed out about certain things? Chances you are. Especially in the world, we're currently living in. It's effortless to be swallowed up in something. It's easy focusing on the negative. You may believe that there's nothing you can do now to change where you are and what you need to do. Stop and think for a moment. If you hate exercise, it's not going to be right at the top of your list of priorities. What do you enjoy doing instead? There has to be something that involves some form of movement. Maybe you enjoy hiking, going for long walks with your beloved pet. That way, you're giving your pet some love and attention while taking care of your physical health at the same time. If you haven't done any exercise for a while, it may be worthwhile starting off small.

Each of these new habits needs to start small, eventually increasing what you're doing in stages until you've reached the point you want to be. Don't overwhelm yourself by attempting to add way too much to the mix all at once. Break your habits into one of the three areas—mental, physical, health. While these three areas may sound simple enough, there are way more challenges than you'd ever thought possible.

Keep Your Mood and Health in Check

What about things to keep your moods and health in check. There are many ways we can change our current eating habits to benefit us in the long run; these range from changing our diet and eating healthier by cutting out junk food and visiting fast-food outlets purely for convenience.

If you find that cooking is taking up a considerable portion of your life during the day, consider doing all the preparation for your meals ahead of time. Sure, you may be spending the more significant part of a day doing this, but if it's going to save you several hours each night, as well as minimizing the amount of wasted food in your home, it's more than worth it. Imagine how much easier it would be to have all your food already prepared for cooking? All you need to do is open whatever freezing method you've used and add it to the pot. Not only will you save hours, but everything is correctly portioned and measured out, just waiting to be cooked.

Apart from working with better meal planning, it's worthwhile visiting each of your medical practitioners regularly. Have them run a complete physical. It could help save your life. Just as you'd take your car in for a service at regular intervals, it's worth taking yourself off to a professional regularly enough that they can pick up whether something's wrong long before the time. I know, I know not everyone has a thing for their medical practitioner. You may be petrified. If you happen to be one of those doomsday people, this is all the more reason to take that leap and have regular checkups. The benefits far outweigh any fear of needles or doctors. Part of the reason we hesitate to go for regular checkups is that we dread receiving bad news. Before the examination, we're already anticipating the worst.

When it comes to receiving a diagnosis that may change your life forever, wouldn't you want to hear about it sooner or later?

Wouldn't you want as much time to get your affairs in order, make peace with those around you, and spend as much time with your loved ones as you can? Maybe the diagnosis is merely a warning—one where you need to become more proactive in taking care of yourself. There's nothing quite like a medical professional telling you that you need to change your eating plan because this will positively affect your life immediately. Let's face it, none of us want to be faced with our mortality, or not now in any event. We'd prefer that everything in our lives is entirely peachy. While this would be ideal, the chances of this happening to us are as slim as our chances to win big on the local lotto.

There are ways to completely mitigate health issues by taking matters into our own hands proactively. Consider your family history of illness. The less you take care of yourself, the higher the risk of you being vulnerable to these diseases. Ensure you have all the necessary tests to ensure that none of these illnesses are lurking in the background. You may not even feel as though there's anything wrong with you. There's no harm in being safe than sorry. There are many tests and examinations that can and should be done depending on your age. If you're unsure which of these tests need to be performed, consult with your medical professional. Once they have all your family medical history, they will consider your age and know what tests they need to run to keep you healthy. When it comes to your health and wellbeing, these are just a couple of things you should be doing.

Try New Things

Stimulate your mental health and wellbeing by trying new things. It can be difficult, especially when you're older and more set in your ways. You're probably thinking to yourself right now, how the hell do I try and learn something new when I've already got so much going on in my life? Part of the reason for this is unless you're constantly learning and growing, your brain ceases to develop and function the way it should. Challenging yourself to step out of your comfort zone can add some excitement to a life that may be incredibly boring. It's once you begin to try new things that you'll appreciate these things. They don't even need to be important things.

Nobody is asking you to get out there and paint a chapel ceiling like Michelangelo, primarily if you've never held a brush in your hands before. However, what's stopping you from taking an art class to begin to learn the very basics of sketching, design, proportion, shapes, colors, and so on. Who knows, this may become one of those things that help you relax. You don't even need to be doing this every day.

If you're uncertain about trying something new, do it anyway. You'll never know who you're going to meet trying to find new things to do. Visit a museum, take yourself off to a museum. Visit the beach of the mountains. You'll never know what's going to become your next best form of stress release unless you give it a go. Not everything you try will become an automatic hit. At least you'll know for next time to avoid those activities.

Finding new things can be a bit of trial and error. There are so many additional benefits to doing this. Especially when you're stuck in a rut, sure, you may love spending time with your family. The truth is that this can become monotonous, and you may crave associating with other adults. Trying to find new, exciting, and brand-new hobbies and activities is one of the ways to do this. We mentioned putting a high-intensity workout into place (this is if you're inclined to enjoy physical fitness.) It might range from simply getting fit to strengthen your core, helping you live a much healthier and happier life. Let's face it, when you feel good about your body, your health automatically improves. Your self-confidence is boosted, along with your self-esteem. It's easier to achieve your goal weight. You need to be cautious of trying to do too much if you haven't been exercising for several years.

You'll have to be patient with yourself, rather than expecting results after the first couple of days. Realistically, it's probably going to take you about a year before you get to where you want to be. Yes, you'll be strengthening your muscles each time you workout but this is going to happen over time. Be realistic with each of your new habits.

When it comes to your mental health, focus on things like taking the time to laugh each day. It's a bit of a cliché saying that laughter is the best medicine but it really is. When last did you have a good laugh at random stuff? If you find it difficult to laugh spontaneously maybe it's worth watching a couple of comedies on a regular basis. Sometimes it pays to find the lighthearted side to things we do and choices we make.

When it comes to existing habits, are there habits and addictions you'd like to change because they're detrimental to your health? If this is the case, then there are a couple of steps that are worth taking. We all know that the first step of any addiction is admitting that you have a problem in the first place. It's is the only way to begin to address anything potentially harmful.

Our habits don't need to include all those huge things that are typically mentioned. Maybe you're in the bad habit of binging on a series or watching movies well into the early hours of the morning. All this is doing is disrupting your sleep patterns. It's not adding any value to your life whatsoever. Chances are you're battling to wake in the morning, or you wake up still feeling tired.

Make a conscious decision to change this habit. One of the things you can do to break this negative cycle is to remove the television from your bedroom. Be sure to stick with the same routine each night.

Now I'm not saying that watching television, series, or movies is a bad thing. I think we all need some form of escape now and then. What I am saying is that when it's done in excess, and it's beginning to interfere with the rest of your life, maybe it's something that needs to be reined in.

Only you will know what moderation is according to your lifestyle. Take into consideration the number of hours you need to sleep each night. Be sure to give yourself enough time to relax before turning in for the night. You will probably have to unplug from the television set between half an hour and an hour before sleeping. Find something else to do that's going to focus your mind without overstimulating it. Some of these things might include reading, journaling, finding something to be grateful for that occurred during the day. Whatever it is, try and develop a habit around each of these things; another reason you want to calm your mind, so you don't have an overactive imagination, especially after watching television programs. It's far too easy for your mind to begin to wander. The last thing you need right before bed is to be focused on what you've just been watching, no matter the content.

Be Mindful of Your Thoughts

Our thoughts can easily take control of our lives and prove to be highly damaging. Trying to control them can be a full-time job. It's not unusual for our thoughts to jump all over the place during the day. Try and avoid this. You want to be able to be in control of where your thoughts go. In control before they go wandering down some random path, distracting you from each of the things you know you should be doing. We've already connected how each of our thoughts can lead to emotions or feelings. It's these emotions and feelings that determine whether we're able to manifest things into our lives.

There is more than enough reason to become way more mindful about where each of our thoughts is taking us. It's time for us to begin to ask some tough questions. Can we shift our emotions from negative to positive instead? Are we mentally tough enough to recognize those emotions keeping us from achieving each of the goals we've identified? Are we strong enough to fail, learn from it, and get right back up again?

Another positive habit of incorporating in our lives is being selective about who you will allow into your social circle. There's no way you can do all of these things on your own. Don't even try. Allow your friends and family to support you through each of these changes. You're doing your best to develop habits that will work with you rather than against you.

Remember that you can do whatever you set your mind to. You can change your life, one single, tiny step at a time. Nothing has to be that big that it seems impossible. There's tremendous value in adding loads of small habits to your day that you can maintain. Go for it. You have absolutely nothing to lose—but everything to gain.

Chapter 10:

Manifesting Abundance

Before even trying to manifest abundance or anything else in your life, you need to have a pretty good idea of precisely what you want. Are you looking for financial freedom, improved relationships, that brand new car you've had your eye on for a while now? Maybe you want a promotion at work, or you're looking at venturing out on your own. Whatever you can identify as being what you want can manifest in your life.

Be careful not to be sending mixed signals to the universe regarding what you want. An excellent example of this is improving your relationships with your spouse, your children, or those you work with. At the same time, you're fighting for that promotion. In this scenario, something's got to give. You know there's no way you can divide yourself in half, trying to accomplish two things that are opposite simultaneously.

Be patient with yourself, especially when things aren't happening quickly enough. It's easy for us to get stuck in that rut where we're comparing where we are to everyone else around us. Life's not a contest, especially against others. As mentioned earlier, because we're individuals, there will always be someone ahead of us.

Living a Life of Abundance

So, what's abundance in any event? It's not always about money. Not that money is bad. It's often an excellent motivator. Let's face it, we all need money to survive. The point of abundance is not just survival. You're looking at finding ways to thrive and to live your best life possible. You want financial problems to go away. Living a life of abundance means that you have way more than you need.

You may be asking whether this isn't greed, probably because that's the way you've been programmed from a young age. The answer to this is no. There's nothing wrong with wanting a better life. There's nothing wrong with finding as many positive solutions as possible that will enhance your life at the moment. Of course, it's not always about money. Many times, we realize there are gaps in our lives that need to be filled.

Maybe we're battling with our health. Our relationships need strengthening, and we're bored, lonely. We no longer feel fulfilled. We're mentally and physically drained. Our lives need some structure, so we feel more in control. Each of these things can be addressed by the law of abundance so long as we're able to focus on the way we think and the subsequent energy we're giving off. How we feel influences how effective the law of abundance is.

Sure, you want to make as many of these things happen as possible. The big question is, do you believe you're deserving of having each of these things. Nothing kills the law of abundance more than doubt and a lack of belief. You have to get to the point where your belief system is unwavering. Any hesitation will influence the outcome. We're so used to living our lives focused on not having things. Changing your mindset can take quite a lot of work before it takes effect. Stop and think about natural disasters, economic downturns, as well as a lack of resources. We become so stuck in the past that looking toward a better future seems futile.

Because of this negative mindset we naturally default to, changing to a focused mindset on abundance isn't always easy. It's going to take a considerable amount of effort and energy. One of the reasons we miss out on the opportunity of taking our futures into our own hands is because we've already decided that we'll never get there. As we learned in the chapter about the Law of Attraction, the universe responds to all this doubt, and that's what manifests in our lives.

There's Power in Thinking Positively

Have you ever met those who seem to have it all without really doing too much about it? Mistakenly, we believe there's something magical about them. We'll notch it up to luck, breeding, an inheritance, and anything else other than making use of the law of abundance. The truth is that they understand exactly how to use this law. They're doing it all the time. You need to understand how to use this law, where your thoughts and attitude are so firmly entrenched in the law of abundance that you no longer even need to think about it. The moment you start thinking that it's something that others can have, you are way down in the pecking order right now. It's something that can never happen to you. You're exactly right. If you want to get there, one of the first things you need to do is banish your vocabulary's negative thinking. Stop thinking that you don't deserve happiness, wealth, health, stronger relationships, the career you dream about, and anything else you can imagine.

The truth is that the moment you get your thinking under control, things will begin to work in your favor.

If you don't believe me, then give it a go. If for one moment you think that it's something that others are born with and developing these skills is way too difficult, I've got news for you. You can learn these skills. Just like anything else in life, the more you practice, the easier it will be for you to begin to manifest whatever abundance you'd like to enjoy.

Let us look back to when you grew up. Depending on how old you are, you may have been raised in a home where you never always had everything you wanted. If you happen to be a Gen Xer, chances are you know what it's like to live through a recession. You've experienced what it feels like to live without luxuries. You need to get past this feeling. So often, we think that the world is overpopulated, and because of this, there's not enough for everyone, but that is utter BS. Of course, there's more than enough for everyone.

Way too often, we're afraid of changing the way we behave. One of the reasons for this is because we're comfortable where we're at. We believe we know it all. We think we're way too old to change anything about our thinking or behavior. So, you may need to learn new ways of doing things, especially when it comes to the way you're thinking. It's this limited thinking that will keep you stuck where you are. Developing an abundance mindset is possible as long as we're prepared to learn.

Let's get back to how we feel about ourselves. The moment we begin to doubt whether we are worthy or deserving of all the good out there, we automatically sabotage all of the good that's just waiting for us to claim it. The next thing you need to do is develop an unwavering belief that everything you want is possible. We are worthy. We deserve to have everything we want out of life. All we have to do is believe it.

If you're in the habit of being jealous of successful people around you, stop it. There's nothing good to come from this negative belief system. Be happy about their success. After all, you have no idea what they've had to do to get there. Be grateful that they're part of your life. You never know when you may have to rely on them to help you work toward your goals. It's far easier for someone who's been there to teach you the ropes than someone who consistently fails. One constant in life is that unless someone has experience or has done whatever they're trying to teach you to do, they're likely to fail horribly.

We limit ourselves from really achieving everything we want out of life by limiting ourselves. We hold back because we don't believe we can achieve, have, or do all the things we want. We think small as a way to test whether the law of abundance works. Small thinking is going to keep us from playing in the big leagues. It's going to keep us from achieving those really big dreams.

We need to be prepared to push those boundaries. Step out of our shell because that's what we want to do. Instead of being afraid to think big, we need to set some goals that almost seem impossible. When it comes to doing this, the only thing is that we need to give ourselves enough time to accomplish what we believe we can. Beware of setting limitations because this will hold you back.

Instead of being hesitant about focusing on abundance, don't you think you should jump right in with both feet? Haven't you been procrastinating for long enough? If you can answer yes to each of these questions, it's time for you to stop playing small and start thinking about those things you deserve. Start working toward them rather than looking for excuses for why you can't have everything you've ever dreamed of.

Changing your entire way of thinking is going to take time. It may mean dealing with fears you have been holding onto. Maybe you've been holding onto them throughout your life so far. Aren't you tired of having the same old things all the time? Aren't you tired of watching those around you succeed, and you are just marking time on the same spot? To be fair, change is hard. It's uncomfortable. It pushes us out of our comfort zone. It isn't as easy as some would have us believe. The reality is that if we want our lives to change, we need to be prepared to do whatever is necessary to make these changes possible.

What we constantly focus on and the way we feel has the power to propel ourselves forward closer to the life we want for ourselves, or it can keep us in that holding pattern. Thinking leads to the way we feel and what we believe. If you're not acutely aware of where your thoughts are going, chances are you can easily get caught up in a sea of negativity. All that's going to accomplish is holding you back.

Visualize Your Goals and Manifest Them

How do you get out of this kind of thinking so you can change where you are at the moment? Because manifesting abundance begins in your mind, that's where you need to begin. You need to be able to visualize what you want in your mind. If you happen to battle with clearly visualizing things mentally, you may need to physically create these images to help you get into the habit of thinking in pictures. For visualization to work, you need to use as many of your senses as possible. It needs to be as authentic as possible.

Suppose you can't close your eyes and imagine everything you want out of life. You're doing something wrong. Without being crystal clear about what you want, it's not likely you'll get what you want from life. If you feel that everything is working against you with any of your goals, you may want to question whether these things are what you want in the first place. If we're uncertain about any of our goals, it may be because we've set ourselves some goals that aren't our own.

Take a look at exactly what goals you've set yourself. The more specific you're able to be about them, the greater your chance of success. Apart from simply trying to visualize your goals clearly, it helps if you write them down. When you do this, don't be afraid to set yourself some time limits. The most important thing when doing this is to be realistic. For instance, don't specify that you're going to get that promotion at work in the next three months if you know you need to complete some courses to qualify. Maybe it's possible in the next 12 months. This is just a simple example of how we place ourselves under pressure by being unrealistic with what we can accomplish in a specific amount of time.

You must balance your life. Balance is one of the main reasons not just concentrating on money, relationships, or your career. There's nothing wrong with any of these things, but try and find a balance. With writing everything down apart from being specific, you should focus on spreading your goals across different areas of your life. Otherwise, the chances are your life is going to feel unfulfilled.

Way too often, we begin working on manifesting abundance, and instead of setting our intention with the universe and leaving it there, we keep on going back. We question ourselves, second-guessing whether we can enjoy the things we've identified. We become fixated on how things will happen instead of concentrating on being specific about what we want. You should be thinking about how you'll feel once you've received what you want instead.

Believe That You Are Worthy of Abundance

Remember that the law of abundance and the universe operate on vibrational energy. You want to be as positive as possible. Suppose you look forward to enjoying what you want, rather than just settling for second best. There's tremendous power in the subconscious mind, and this is one of the key reasons it's so important to get to the point where you're no longer consciously fixated on your goals. You want to give your subconscious time to work with the universe.

It's not always clear exactly how all of this works, but it does. Remember to think in positive tense all the time. The moment your self-talk becomes negative, that's what the universe hears. It becomes part of the vibrational energy you project, and of course, it's what manifests. You must ditch your negative thinking and belief system for those that are positive instead.

Negative self-talk and limiting beliefs are two significant components that will keep you stuck where you are indefinite. Remember the belief that there isn't enough to go around. As soon as you start believing this, you're setting yourself up for this to become your reality. Give up each of these beliefs because subconsciously, you're transferring this negative energy. You're allowing this to determine your future.

When it comes to money, we can easily get caught up in believing that only certain people have it in them to be wealthy. The problem with thinking this is that it questions our self-worth. We connect the way we feel about ourselves directly to the amount of money we have in the bank. Of course, this is all nonsense. We sell ourselves short. We believe that others are way better than us because they're wealthy. We judge and criticize ourselves.

What we say out loud and what we think internally can impact us positively or negatively. Remember each of those emotions that we feel. They're ultimately responsible for everything that happens in our lives. Whether we're successful or fail, it's all due to our self-talk and the beliefs we have about ourselves.

It's important to recognize that we have the ability and the power to attract anything we desire into our lives. All we have to do is firmly believe that we're worthy of enjoying, owning, or becoming whatever we want. The secret is acknowledging that whatever we want is out there, just waiting for us. It's understanding and accepting that each of the words we utter or even think can hold power to determine our future.

Believe me that being positive all the time is hard work. Will it all be worth it in the end? That's an indisputable yes. When things get complicated, and they will do, it's crucial to keep going. No matter how you may be feeling at the time. You should get to the point where giving in is not an option. Not if you want to be enjoying all the benefits that abundance has to offer.

As you begin to see positive things occurring in your life, don't forget to express gratitude. Gratitude is one of the most potent emotions next to love that you should be striving to make part of your life. The whole law of abundance hinges entirely on how we feel emotionally. It's one thing to think about things.

It's entirely different from actually feeling. Belief without emotions won't work.

You are worthy of everything you dream about. As you receive each of things, express gratitude to the universe for granting you the desires of your heart. Keep track of each of these things so that the next time you're feeling downhearted, you'll have something positive to reflect on, giving you the power to shift your emotional state from where you know you shouldn't be to where you want to be.

Conclusion

Life has a way of throwing so many negative things in our direction, making it more than challenging to come to terms with where we are at. Of course, there is no guarantee that things are suddenly going to get easier. We not only have conventional challenges we need to overcome, but we have mental and physical challenges that are unique to each of us.

Depending on where we are in our lives, some of these challenges can be more trying than others. Regardless of where they fall on the spectrum of our lives, they are there, and we have to figure out the best possible way of moving beyond each of them. It is easy trying to emulate those around us. Unfortunately, this has a direct impact on our authenticity. Without this level of authenticity, chances are we'll spend most of our lives questioning not only our behavior but the motivation behind each decision.

Sure, we all want to be successful. What exactly does that mean? Because it's so individual, it is too difficult to find a definition that covers all the bases. I guess it is one of the few ways you can finally say you have achieved everything you want from life and are happy with where you are. You are comfortable in your skin, not worrying about anything others may feel about you or your attitude toward you. Granted, none of this is easy to do. You will have to work your way through some tough challenges. That is not to say you can't do it. All that it means is that you may need to come to terms with the fact that you have way more to do than dream about the future.

After all, there is nothing out there that is more important than being able to fulfill your destiny.

Dreaming is one thing, but it requires a great deal of action before it becomes a reality, before it becomes something real enough for you to make the sacrifice necessary to become motivated to take things to the next level. Without this motivation, you are probably dead in the water. Choose the path of honesty and integrity instead of simply going with the flow.

It is much easier to follow the crowd; this will not bring you any closer to achieving your ultimate goals. Remember the collation between those things your mind perceives to be actual reality. Are you firmly fixed on being able to create the kind of future you know you deserve or are you still putting up barriers? Are you still looking for all the excuses why you should not be making a move to improve your life?

One of the most important things you can do for yourself right now is being aware of who you are deep down. Following this intuition can direct you to where you need to go rather than holding you back or hindering your progress. It is vital throughout this whole experience for you to remain true to who you are. Why should you change who you are, especially when pleasing others or satisfying their agenda?

Admittedly, we often find it much easier to appease those around us rather than becoming all-consumed with taking control of our own lives. You want to be able to say that you've done it all on your own, that you have been able to make your luck, especially when those around you believe that it is all down to luck rather than effort. We all know that this premise is faulty.

The only person that has total control over the beliefs they hold true and exactly what they do with this truth is us. Isn't it time to admit that everything we have ever wanted is within our reach? All that is required is to have the belief system and the courage to go after exactly what we want. It means choosing everything from this badass menu called life.

Stop limiting your progress in this life with all the stories you keep telling yourself. Stories meant to scare you from even trying. Stories that you don't deserve to be there. Stories that you have no control over your destiny because it has already been written. Do you know how insane this sounds?

The question you need to ask yourself is how badly you want success. How badly do you want a life by design, rather than one that is left to society or fate? In each chapter, there have been various simple techniques to help you accomplish any goal you set yourself.

Turn your current negative self-talk into something way more positive. You want to spur yourself on, closer toward the objectives you set yourself, rather than dragging yourself down with negativity. Realize that there is no way you will be able to do these things on your own. Make use of the techniques outlined in this book.

No matter how many times you choose to refer back to these chapters, know that, you have the power to take control of your own life. If you are willing to put in the effort, whatever your heart desires can be yours. It doesn't matter whether it is health, happiness, wealth, career success, or strengthening relationships with others.

Whatever it is that you are after, you can shape your future by using the tools provided. You can finally live a life of abundance. You can have, do or become anything you want to. All you have to do is believe.

References

Abber, C. (2019, January 24). *How to actually forgive yourself.* Oprah Daily. https://www.oprahdaily.com/life/a26028888/how-to-forgive-yourself/

Abundance No Limits. (n.d.). *What Are The 7 Laws of Attraction?* Abundance No Limits. https://www.abundancenolimits.com/what-are-the-7-laws-of-attraction/

Andras, S. (2021, February 4). *7 Ways to find out what you really want in life.* Lifehack. https://www.lifehack.org/articles/communication/7-ways-find-out-what-you-really-want-life.html

Beohm, R. (2018, May 8). *Change vs. Growth.* Medium. https://rachelforte.medium.com/change-vs-growth-8abfbe69d091

Blush Life Coaching. (2021, January 7). *What self-love is, why it's so important and how to make it part of your daily routine.* SUCCESS. https://www.success.com/why-self-love-is-important-and-how-to-practice-it/

Borenstein, J. (2020, February 12). *Self-Love and what it means.* Brain & Behavior Research Foundation. https://www.bbrfoundation.org/blog/self-love-and-what-it-means

Buice, D. (2017, September 27). *7 Healthy habits for a healthy life.* Living Magazine. https://www.livingmagazine.net/7-healthy-habits-healthy-life/

Burns, C. L. (n.d.). *What happens when you finally realize you deserve better.* Thriveglobal.com. https://thriveglobal.com/stories/what-happens-when-you-finally-realize-you-deserve-better/

Canfield, J. (2015, March 16). *Utilizing the law of attraction.* Jackcanfield. https://www.jackcanfield.com/blog/utilizing-the-law-of-attraction/

Canfield, J. (2019, January 2). *Using the law of attraction for joy, relationships, money & more [Guide].* America's Leading Authority on Creating Success and Personal Fulfillment - Jack Canfield. https://www.jackcanfield.com/blog/using-the-law-of-attraction/

Caprino, K. (2019, August 18). *4 Ways to take accountability for your actions (and why so many don't).* Forbes. https://www.forbes.com/sites/kathycaprino/2019/08/18/4-ways-to-take-accountability-for-your-actions-and-why-so-many-dont/

Cherry, K. (2021, February 17). *How to forgive yourself*. Verywell Mind. https://www.verywellmind.com/how-to-forgive-yourself-4583819

Cherry, K. (2020, April 29). *What is the negativity bias?* Verywell Mind. https://www.verywellmind.com/negative-bias-4589618

Christ, S. (2021, February 4). *7 Powerful questions to find out what you want to do with your life*. Lifehack. https://www.lifehack.org/articles/communication/7-powerful-questions-find-out-what-you-want-with-your-life.html

Cohen, J. (2018, December 4). *Surrounding yourself with the right people changes everything*. Forbes. https://www.forbes.com/sites/jennifercohen/2018/12/04/surrounding-yourself-with-the-right-people-changes-everything/

Cory, T. L., & Platt, C. (2021). *What is a toxic relationship? - 8 Types of toxic relationships and their signs*. HealthScope. https://healthscopemag.com/health-scope/toxic-relationships/

Daskal, L. (2018, February 15). *How to accept yourself, your life, and your reality*. Inc.com; Inc. https://www.inc.com/lolly-daskal/how-to-accept-yourself-your-life-your-reality.html

Flaxington, B. D. (2019, January 17). *The importance of self-love | Psychology Today South Africa*. Www.psychologytoday.com. https://www.psychologytoday.com/za/blog/understand-other-people/201901/the-importance-self-love

Fritscher, L. (2020, June 20). *The psychology of fear*. Verywell Mind; Verywellmind. https://www.verywellmind.com/the-psychology-of-fear-2671696

Frothingham, S. (2019, December 17). *Do you have a negativity bias?* Healthline. https://www.healthline.com/health/negativity-bias

Goldstein, J. (2014, April 25). *7 Lies you keep telling yourself that hold you back from growing*. Lifehack. https://www.lifehack.org/articles/communication/7-lies-you-keep-telling-yourself-that-hold-you-back-from-growing/html

Haniff, S. (2017, January 13). *7 Reasons it's important to surround yourself with positive people*. WomenWorking. https://www.womenworking.com/7-reasons-important-surround-positive-people/

Health Scotland. (2021, April 14). *Ten ways to fight your fears*. Www.nhsinform.scot. https://www.nhsinform.scot/healthy-living/mental-wellbeing/fears-and-phobias/ten-ways-to-fight-your-fears

Hunt, E. (2020, March 11). *What's the secret of happiness? Accepting that life is messy and difficult.* The Guardian. https://www.theguardian.com/music/shortcuts/2020/mar/11/as-ellie-goulding-knows-accepting-life-is-messy-is-the-key-to-happiness

Jacobs, C. (2021, April 1). *Why is self love important? - UpJourney.* UpJourney. https://upjourney.com/why-is-self-love-important

James, M. (2014, October 22). *How to forgive yourself and move on from the past | Psychology Today South Africa.* Www.psychologytoday.com. https://www.psychologytoday.com/za/blog/focus-forgiveness/201410/how-forgive-yourself-and-move-the-past

James, M. (2015, May 17). *6 Signs that fear is holding you back.* Psychology Today. https://www.psychologytoday.com/us/blog/focus-forgiveness/201505/6-signs-fear-is-holding-you-back

Jaworski, M. (2020, February 19). *The negativity bias: Why the bad stuff sticks and how to overcome it.* Psycom.net - Mental Health Treatment Resource since 1986. https://www.psycom.net/negativity-bias

Jensen, M. (2021, January 12). *Your life is a mess? How to fix it and turn things around.* Lifehack.

https://www.lifehack.org/827423/my-life-is-a-mess

Kruse, K. (2020, January 13). *Improve personal accountability: 12 things to do in 12 weeks.* Forbes. https://www.forbes.com/sites/kevinkruse/2020/01/13/improve-personal-accountability-12-things-to-do-in-12-weeks/

Lindberg, S. (2018, July 25). *12 Tips for forgiving yourself.* Healthline. https://www.healthline.com/health/how-to-forgive-yourself

Logothetis, L. (2017, December 6). *Keeping good company: Why you should surround yourself with good people.* HuffPost. https://www.huffpost.com/entry/kkeeping-good-company-why-you-should-surround-yourself-with-good-people_b_6816468

Luke, A. (2009, June 11). *The difference between change and growth - and knowing which you need.* Possibility Change. https://possibilitychange.com/the-difference-between-change-and-growth-and-knowing-which-you-need/

Mason, T. (2021, January 21). *4 Simple steps to track your progress towards your goals.* Lifehack. https://www.lifehack.org/articles/productivity/4-ways-track-your-progress-toward-your-goals.html

Matthews, D. (2020, December 9). *How to identify your limiting beliefs and get over them.* Lifehack. https://www.lifehack.org/858652/limiting-beliefs

Moore, C. (2019, December 30). *What is the negativity bias and how can it be overcome?* PositivePsychology.com. https://positivepsychology.com/3-steps-negativity-bias/

Nicole, T. (2017, December 4). *Lies you tell yourself that are holding you back from living your best life.* Tiffany Nicole Forever. http://tiffanynicoleforever.com/2017/12/lies-you-tell-yourself/

Patel, D. (2019, March 6). *8 Ways to stay accountable with your goals.* Entrepreneur. https://www.entrepreneur.com/article/328070

Paul - Self Help for Life. (2020, July 14). *The 10 steps to manifesting abundance and prosperity.* Self Help for Life. https://selfhelpforlife.com/manifesting-abundance-and-prosperity/

Pullein, C. (2021, June 7). *6 Golden rules to make progress towards achieving goals.* Lifehack; Lifehack. https://www.lifehack.org/articles/productivity/6-simple-steps-to-make-progress-towards-achieving-a-goal.html

Rettig, T. (2017, December 7). *Belief systems: what they are and how they affect you*. Medium; Intercultural Mindset. https://medium.com/intercultural-mindset/belief-systems-what-they-are-and-how-they-affect-you-1cd87aa775ff

Robbins, T. (n.d.). *Law of attraction: The complete guide from Tony*. Tonyrobbins.com. https://www.tonyrobbins.com/business/law-of-attraction/

Salem, C. (2017, September 4). *Why being accountable is important? | Christopher Salem*. Christopher Salem. https://christophersalem.com/why-being-accountable-is-important/

Sargent, K. (2014, April 10). *12 Things you do that are holding you back from success*. Lifehack. https://www.lifehack.org/articles/productivity/12-things-you-that-are-holding-you-back-from-success.html

Scott, E. (2020, November 18). *Understanding and using the law of attraction in your life*. Verywell Mind; Verywellmind. https://www.verywellmind.com/understanding-and-using-the-law-of-attraction-3144808

Scott, E. (2021, January 26). *Maintaining Healthy Habits - In 5 Simple steps*. Verywell Mind. https://www.verywellmind.com/maintainting-healthy-habits-3144721

Scott, S. (2019, February 8). *192 Health habits: A simple list of healthy living habits*. Develop Good Habits. https://www.developgoodhabits.com/healthy-habits/

Siggins, K. (2016, April 18). *HOW TO BE PERSONALLY ACCOUNTABLE | Kerry Siggins |blog*. Kerry Siggins. https://kerrysiggins.com/blog/how-to-be-personally-accountable-and-why-its-so-important/

Stewart, A. R. (2017, November 17). *13 Habits of self-love every woman should adopt*. Healthline. https://www.healthline.com/health/13-self-love-habits-every-woman-needs-to-have

Suttie, J. (2020, January 13). *How to overcome your brain's fixation on bad things*. Greater Good. https://greatergood.berkeley.edu/article/item/how_to_overcome_your_brains_fixation_on_bad_things

Team Tony. (2018, January 30). *Fear: the biology behind it and how to leverage your fear*. Tonyrobbins.com. https://www.tonyrobbins.com/mind-meaning/what-are-you-afraid-of/

Wakeman, C. (2015, October 26). *Personal accountability and the pursuit of workplace happiness*. Forbes. https://www.forbes.com/sites/cywakeman/201

5/10/26/personal-accountability-and-the-pursuit-of-workplace-happiness/

Walsh, R. (2020, May 26). *The lies that hold us back.* Medium. https://rachel-walsh.medium.com/the-lies-that-hold-us-back-7cb997b04031

WomensMedia. (2021, March 9). *How to step out of negativity: 7 Tips.* Forbes. https://www.forbes.com/sites/womensmedia/2021/03/09/how-to-step-out-of-negativity-7-tips/

Wood, K. (2016, December 15). *11 Ways to understand the law of attraction & how to use it to get what you want.* Bustle. https://www.bustle.com/articles/198708-11-ways-to-understand-the-law-of-attraction-how-to-use-it-to-get-what

Young, K. (2016, April 20). *15 Signs of a toxic relationship.* Heysigmund.com. https://www.heysigmund.com/toxic-relationship-15-signs/

Young, K. (2017, June 5). *Here's how to make DAILY progress toward your goals.* Medium. https://medium.com/the-mission/heres-how-to-make-daily-progress-toward-your-goals-9e804bdd9d76

Printed in Great Britain
by Amazon